A TASTE OF NATURE
Edible Plants of the Southwest
And How to Prepare Them
<<<<<>>>>>

A TASTE OF NATURE
Edible Plants of the Southwest
And How to Prepare Them

<<<<<>>>>>

Written and Illustrated by
Kahanah Farnsworth

A TASTE OF NATURE
Third Edition

Library of Congress #2004098220

Farnsworth, Kahanah, 1946—
A taste of nature: edible plants of the Southwest and how to prepare them/written and illustrated by Kahanah Farnsworth
p. cm.
Includes bibliographical references and index.
ISBN # 0-9644605-1-3
1. Cookery (Wild foods)
2. Wild plants, EdibleóSouthwe stern States. I. Title
TX823.F39 1996
641/6—dc20
96-35789   CIP

Printed in the United States of America by
Patterson Printing
Benton Harbor, Michigan

"And God said, Behold, I have given you every herb bearing seed, which is upon the face of all the earth, and every tree, in which is the fruit of a tree yielding seed; to you it shall be for meat."

Genesis 1:29

CONTENTS

COLOR SECTION..................157

PART II
Poisonous Plants

INTRODUCTION

This handbook is designed to be reader-friendly. All of the plants have been selected for their availability, easy recognition, and their usefulness. When there is the possibility of confusing an edible plant with a poisonous one, the differences between the two are clearly indicated. The recipes in *A Taste of Nature* have been eaten and enjoyed by people of all ages. If you find a favorite recipe but lack a specific plant you can often substitute a similar one in its place. (There is a list of possible plant substitutes on page 198). Learning about and using plants is as exciting as searching for hidden treasure. As always, please use common sense. Avoid; picking endangered plants, uprooting plants when you only need to harvest a few leaves, and eating plants which have been sprayed or grow in an unhealthy environment. So, have fun – happy foraging and bon appétit!

* There is no such thing as the exact size of a plant or the precise season in which it grows. Plants are influenced by many factors: their geographic location, the altitude and climate where they grow, how near they are to water, and if they are shaded or in the sun. Consequently, although the statistics and seasons given in this book are generally accurate, there are always exceptions. For example; plants that are available during late winter in southern California may not appear until several months later at a higher altitude or in a northern climate.

PART I

Edible Plants and Their Recipes

AMARANTH

Amaranthus retroflexus

Pigweed, Redroot, Quelite

Features: *A. retroflexus* is an annual which first appears during late spring and early summer. It can reach a height of 4 feet but is usually much shorter. Its pale green, ovate leaves have pointed tips and grow in clusters alternately along stems and branches. Tiny, densely packed, green flowers grow at the ends of stems and branches as well as at their juncture. The taproot is often red.

Facts: Amaranth grows throughout the United States in moist locations and waste places*. The best time to gather it is while the plants are young and tender. Amaranth seeds and leaves are high in calcium and very nutritious. However, amaranth has a tendency to accumulate nitrates from soil, and should be eaten in moderation if harvested in an area where nitrate fertilizers are used. All amaranths produce copious quantities of seeds which were used by Native Americans for bread and mush, or just parched and eaten. When the seeds are heated, they supposedly pop like small kernels of popcorn.

Foods:
Raw: Amaranth leaves can be eaten as a snack or added to salads and sandwiches.

Cooked: They can be boiled, steamed, sautéed, stir-fried, or added to soups and stews. Because these leaves have a mild flavor, they can be used in most recipes that call for cooked greens.

SAVORY PASTRIES
(Makes 8 pastries)

> 3/4 cup chopped amaranth greens, lightly steamed
> 1/2 cup grated Parmesan
> 2 green onions, chopped
> 1 egg, beaten
> 1 tube refrigerated crescent roll dough

Preheat the oven to 400° F. Press cooked greens into a sieve with the back of a spoon to remove all excess liquid. Combine greens with cheese, onions and about half of the beaten egg. Carefully unroll dough and separate it into triangles. Gently stretch each triangle so that it is more or less equilateral. To fill; place a triangle of dough in front of you so that it is pointing away from you. Put 1/8 of the filling in the middle of the triangle, then bring both the right and the left points to the top point and press the seams together. Transfer the finished triangles to an ungreased cookie sheet. Brush them with the remainder of the beaten egg. Bake until well-browned on top.

(Reprinted by permission from *The Tumbleweed Gourmet* by Carolyn Niethammer, 1987, the University of Arizona Press, Tucson, Arizona).

*Waste places refer to disturbed ground and roadsides.

AMARANTH, #2

Amaranthus palmeri

Features: *A. palmeri* is a dark green annual that can grow either erect or prostrate. Its leaves are darker above than beneath, and grow alternately along ridged stems and stiff pale green branches. The lower leaves are larger than those higher up, so from a distance, the silhouette of this amaranth appears pyramid-like. Inconspicuous green flowers and an abundance of tiny black seeds grow in dense, bristly, whorled spikes at the ends of stems and branches and at the junctures of leaves and branches. On older plants the main stem and tips of the leaves often turn a bright rose-red. Most plants grow to be 12 to 18 inches high.

Facts: All amaranths are edible and similar in taste. Young plants are the tenderest. *A. palmeri* can be found growing throughout the United States, especially in waste places. It matures later in summer than *A. retroflexus* and is smaller, with lighter colored leaves.

Foods:
Raw: Amaranth leaves are mild and can be eaten raw in sandwiches and salads.

Cooked: The whole plant can be steamed, boiled, stir-fried, or sautéed.

MINESTRONE
(Serves 4 – 6)

> 2 tablespoons extra virgin olive oil
> 2 cloves garlic, minced
> 1 onion, chopped
> 4 tomatoes, diced
> 4 cups water
> 1/2 cup pasta
> 3 potatoes, diced

3 large carrots, sliced
2 stalks celery, sliced
1 cup green beans
1/2 cup peas
1/2 cup cooked white beans
2 cups amaranth leaves, chopped
1/2 teaspoon basil
1 teaspoon oregano
2 teaspoons salt
1/4 teaspoon pepper
2 cups water (optional)

Heat oil in a large pot. Sauté onion and garlic until clear. Add tomatoes and cook for several minutes, stirring occasionally. Then add the rest of the ingredients except seasonings and final 2 cups of water. Cover and bring to a boil. Lower heat and simmer for at least 1/2 hour. Then stir in seasonings and 2 final cups of water (optional). Heat for 5 minutes and serve.

ARTEMISIAS

Sagebrush *Artemisia californica*

Mugwort *A. douglasiana*

Wormwood *A. palmeri*

Features: All artemisias are very aromatic. Sagebrush is not a sage but an annual evergreen shrub which grows up to 6 feet tall. Its small, narrow, grayish-green leaves are once or twice parted and grow alternately in small clusters along flexible gray-green branches. Older plants become rigid and woody at their bases. Tiny yellow flowers grow in long clusters from the ends of the branches. Mugwort grows 2 to 3 feet high. Several stems cluster together at ground level, often branching near the top of the stems. There are many different species of mugwort. *A. douglasiana* has alternate leaves which are dark green above and almost silver beneath. These narrow, pointed leaves decrease in size as they approach the tips of the branches. The larger leaves, which grow lower on the stems, are sometimes irregularly notched.
Wormwood, a many-branched perennial herb, grows up to 6 1/2 feet high. Its new branches are slender and flexible, but the base of the plant becomes woody with age. Both mugwort and wormwood have ridged stems. Wormwood's abundant leaves are almost fern-like in appearance. Delicate and slender, each leaf is parted one or more times on each side.

Facts: Sagebrush is found mostly in chaparral* communities throughout the West. Mugwort grows in diverse habitats: mountains, canyons, and moist arroyos along the Pacific Coast. The variety of wormwood known as *Artemisia palmeri* is fairly rare, so please don't pick it unless necessary. Many varieties of wormwood are found throughout the world. Although both mugwort and wormwood can be gathered at any time of the year, sagebrush is most potent when collected during summer.

Artemisias are natural bug repellents. Native Americans frequently lined their acorn storage baskets with these plants in order to protect their acorns from bugs. Mugwort is also used as a moth repellent. Teas can be brewed from most artemisias, but they tend to be bitter unless limited amounts of leaves are steeped for a short period of time. These teas are generally useful in promoting sweating or as an aid in cases of indigestion.

Foods:
Tea: Use only a small portion of 1 leaf for mugwort or wormwood tea. For sagebrush tea, use several leaves. Place the leaves in a cup. Fill with boiling water. Cover and steep for 5 minutes. Strain, sweeten and serve. These teas can be used medicinally, but are not recommended for people with emphysema or bronchitis, or during pregnancy.

Sagebrush

*Chaparral communities are those "comprising shrubby plants widely distributed in southern California that are especially adapted to dry sunny summers and moist winters." (Webster's Third New International Dictionary [Springfield, MA: Merriam Webster, 1986]).

Mugwort   Wormwood

AUSTRALIAN SALTBUSH

Atriplex semibaccata

Features: There are over 30 varieties of atriplex in California alone. Australian saltbush is a low-growing mat-like perennial that spreads out from a central taproot. It can grow up to 1 foot tall; but unless it is climbing up a fence or barrier, is usually much shorter. *A. semibaccata* has many pale, slender, wand-like stems, several branches, and small, stiff, oblong leaves which grow alternately along stems in small bundles. Pale green on top and light beneath, the leaves appear to be dusted with white powder. Tiny red berries with pointed ends appear during late spring and summer.

Facts: Australian saltbush can be gathered year-round but is most tender in spring. This prolific plant thrives throughout California in the poor, dry soil that is found in saline waste areas and along roadsides. Both plant and berries are edible and can be used as a salty seasoning for other foods. Native Americans used to gather the seeds, grind them, and use them for flour.

Foods:
Raw: The crisp berries, small leaves, and stems can be eaten raw or added to salads. Although the tiny berries are juicy, they are not very refreshing because of their salinity.

Cooked: Australian saltbush leaves can be added to other greens or cooked with meat. Be sure to sample the finished food before you add salt.

CURRIED SPLIT PEA SOUP
(Serves 6 – 10)

This delicious soup requires little preparation, but takes several hours to cook.

> 1 pound split peas, cleaned
> 4 cups water

1 tablespoon extra virgin olive oil
2-3 cloves garlic, minced
1 onion, copped
2 stalks celery, sliced
1 cup grated carrots
4 cups water
2 cups saltbush leaves
1 1/2 teaspoons salt
1/4 teaspoon pepper
1/2 teaspoon curry powder

Put split peas and 4 cups of water into a large pot. Bring to a boil. Then lower the heat and simmer for 1 hour. Transfer peas and liquid into a bowl. Heat olive oil in the same pot and sauté garlic and onion until clear. Add celery and carrots and heat for 2 to 3 minutes, stirring occasionally. Add the other 4 cups of water and bring to a boil. Stir in saltbush leaves, seasonings, and cooked split peas. Cover, bring to a boil, and lower the heat. Simmer until soup is thick— about 1 hour or more. Serve with hot, crusty sourdough bread.

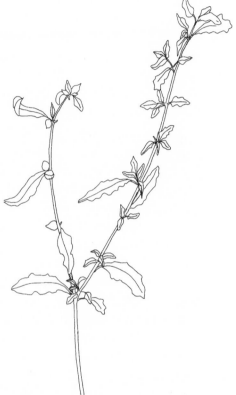

BLACK SAGE

Salvia mellifera

Features: Black Sage is an aromatic perennial shrub that grows 3 to 6 feet tall. Numerous slightly curved branches give the entire bush a rounded appearance. Its square stems are often faded red when young, but darken with age. Small dark green leaves grow in pairs, each pair facing in a different direction from the pair above and the one below. At the juncture of leaf and stem are shorter stems with clusters of smaller leaves. Delicate, pale periwinkle-blue flowers appear in spring, growing in dense tiered whorls along the ends of slender branches. Black sage leaves emit a pleasant mint-like odor when crushed.

Facts: Black sage grows on sunny chaparral hillsides and in coastal sage scrub communities in southern California. This is the sage that was used by early settlers to season sausage, poultry, and stuffing. White sage and sagebrush are much too strong to use in this manner. Nutritious black sage seeds were gathered and used for food by Native Americans. Cahuillas used to parch the seeds and grind them to make meal. Various Native American tribes used a rinse made from black sage leaves to maintain the color of their hair. Although one friend of mine did not see a significant difference in hair color after rinsing with black sage tea, others have claimed that their hair became darker when they rubbed the sage water into their scalp 2 to 3 times a week and did not immediately rinse it out. Either way, sage rinse adds a shine to hair and an elusive woodsy scent.

Foods:
Tea: Crush 1/2 leaf and place it into a cup. Add boiling water. Cover and steep for 5 minutes. Strain, sweeten, and serve. In the past, black sage tea was used as a gargle for sore throats and applied topically as a disinfectant. When used medicinally, black sage is usually gathered while in flower and then dried and bundled.

Cooked: The leaves can be used for flavoring soups, stews, and stuffing. Remember to use them in moderation - a little goes a long way.

GAZPACHO WITH SAGE
(Serves 2 – 4)

> 4 tomatoes, diced
> 1 clove garlic, minced
> 1/4 onion, sliced
> 1 stalk celery, chopped
> 1/4 green pepper, diced
> 1/2 cucumber, peeled and cut
> 1 tablespoon lemon juice
> 1/2 teaspoon salt
> Dash cayenne pepper
> 1/2 black sage leaf
> Several sprigs of cilantro

Liquefy tomatoes in a blender. Blend in all the other ingredients except cilantro. Pour into serving bowls, refrigerate. Then garnish each with a sprig of cilantro and serve cold for a refreshing treat.

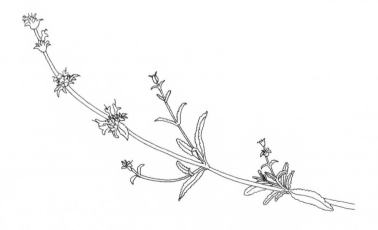

BLACKBERRY

Rubus ursinus

Bramble Bush, Pacific Blackberry

Features: Blackberry bushes usually grow in thickets 5 to 10 feet high, but sometimes are trailing vines up to 7 feet long. The leaves of *R. ursinus* grow in sets of three leaflets, all of which have sharply serrated margins. As the leaves approach the tips of the branches, their leaflets sometimes appear to merge together, forming a single 2 or 3-lobed leaf. All parts of blackberry bushes are covered with sharp thorns. The flowers have 5 fragile white petals and are followed by small, hard, lumpy berries which are first green, then red, and finally become black and juicy as they ripen. People often confuse blackberry bushes with poison oak because they have similar leaves and both prefer moist environments. However, blackberry bushes clearly have thorns, whereas poison oak does not.

Facts: Blackberry bushes thrive near streambeds and in other moist locations throughout the United States. The berries ripen during summer. Remember to wear old clothes when picking blackberries because the juice will stain your clothes if it gets on them. Blackberries are a good source of vitamin C. Native Americans dried the berries to preserve them. They also mixed fresh blackberries with meat and fat to make pemmican. A tea made from the roots was used by northern California Indians as a cure for diarrhea.

Foods:
Tea: A mild tea can be made from the leaves. (Only use dry leaves, never damp ones). Put 3 or 4 crumbled leaves into a cup. Add boiling water. Cover and steep for 10 minutes. Strain, sweeten, and serve.

Raw: Delicious blackberries can be added to fruit salads or smoothies. Young shoots are also edible raw.

Cooked: Blackberries can be made into jams, jellies, pies, and syrups, or added to pancakes and waffles. Young stems can be boiled, steamed, or stir-fried.

BLACKBERRY JAM OR SYRUP
(Makes about 3 pints)

> 8 cups ripe blackberries, cleaned
> 1 cup apple juice
> 1 package pectin
> 3 cups sugar

Mash berries and apple juice together in a pot. Stir in pectin. Bring to a rolling boil and boil gently for 30 to 60 minutes, stirring constantly. Add sugar and boil for 1 minute more. Remove jam and pour into sterilized containers. It will continue to thicken as it cools. After the jam is cool, cover and refrigerate for immediate use or freeze for future use. If you want syrup, remove the mixture before it gets too thick.

BUCKWHEAT

Eriogonum fasciculatum

Flat-Topped Buckwheat

Features: Flat-topped buckwheat is a much-branched plant whose stiff stems first appear in late winter. They are adorned with small bundles of rosemary-like leaves. By May or June, buckwheat is 2 to 3 feet high and topped by compound umbels of small pinkish-white flowers that become reddish-brown as they age. The seeds are also reddish-brown. Buckwheat is often confused with chamise *(Adenostoma fasciculatum)*, which has small pointed leaves growing along its brittle stems and branches. However, chamise is a larger bush, has slightly larger leaves which are not as dense, and its small white flowers grow in terminal clusters, whereas buckwheat's flowers grow in compound umbels.

Facts: Buckwheat is common to chaparral communities of the West. It should be gathered in May or June when it flowers.

Foods:
Tea: Put 3 tablespoon of flowers into a cup. Fill with boiling water. Cover and steep for 5 minutes. Strain, sweeten, and serve. This tea is said to be good for high blood pressure and bronchial ailments. If

you replace the flowers with 2 tablespoons of leaves, the resulting tea is reputed to alleviate headaches and stomach pains. For bladder trouble, tea made with 2 tablespoons of combined stems and leaves is recommended.

BUCKWHEAT BREAD
(Makes 1 loaf)

> 1 cup warm water
> 1 package yeast
> 1 tablespoon sugar
> 1 teaspoon salt
> 1 tablespoon oil
> 2 cups unbleached flour
> 1/4 cup buckwheat flowers, crushed

Combine water, yeast and sugar. Cover with a warm, moist dish towel and let rise in a warm place until puffy. Add salt, oil and 1 cup flour. Cover and let rise until doubled in size—about 1 hour. Then add the second cup of flour and the buckwheat flowers. Knead the dough and add more flour if necessary to keep it from sticking. Shape into a loaf and place in a greased loaf pan. Cover; let rise in a warm place until doubled in size, then bake at 350° for 50 minutes or until done.

BULRUSH

Scirpus acutus

Tule

Features: Bulrushes have hollow unbranched stems which grow 4 to 12 feet tall with brown bristly flowers and seed-like fruit growing in small drooping clusters at the top of each stem. Long, narrow, pointed leaves grow vertically from the base of the plants. There are about 20 different species of bulrushes in the West alone. Some species have triangular-shaped stems, but those of *Scirpus acutus* are round.

Facts: Bulrushes grow in or along streams, ponds, and lake edges. Because they are very nutritious, they were an important food plant for Native Americans. Locations where cattails and bulrushes grow are often thought of as natural "supermarkets" because of all the foods these two plants provide. Their leaves are also useful. Native Americans used them to make mats and settlers used them to cane chairs.

Foods:
Raw: In spring, young bulrush shoots can be peeled and eaten raw. The part nearest the base is best. It's white with a crunchy celery-like texture. Stem bases immediately above the roots and the rhizomes can also be eaten raw and are most tender when young. Later on, pollen can be gathered from the mature flowers, before the seeds are available. Rootstocks can be collected year-round.

Cooked: The rhizomes can be boiled, baked, steamed or roasted. Bulrush pollen can be gathered by shaking the flower heads into a bag. After the pollen is cleaned, it can be used 1/2 and 1/2 with regular flour in recipes calling for flour. The seeds can be gathered, ground, and used to make flour or gruel.

BULRUSH SALAD
(Serves 3)

>   1/2 cup bulrush bases, cleaned
>   and chopped
>   1/2 cup tomatoes, diced
>   1/4 cup Bermuda onion, minced
>   1/4 cup green pepper, diced

Mix together and serve with a vinaigrette
salad dressing. (See page 77).

CATTAIL

Typha latifolia

Features: This perennial plant spreads by underground rhizomes. Each spring new shoots, called "Cossack Asparagus," appear. Cattail stalks grow from 4 to 8 feet tall. Green flower spikes, which form near the top of these stalks, turn brown as they mature, then become covered with yellow pollen. In summer, when cattails go to seed, the flower spikes are covered with white down. Long, slender, green, grass-like leaves grow alternately along the stalks, often extending higher than the flower spikes.

Facts: Cattails can be found in streams, ponds, and lakes year-round. During World War II, when supplies were low, cattail fluff called "kapok" was used to fill life jackets and cheap sleeping bags. Kapok floats and is waterproof. Cattail leaves can be used to make rush chair seats, floor mats, and roofing thatch.

Foods:
Raw: White and crispy, pleasantly mild in flavor, the young, peeled shoots and crowns can be eaten raw or added to salads.

Cooked: New cattail shoots can be steamed or boiled. The green flower spikes can be boiled and served like corn on the cob. Cattail rhizomes, which are rich in carbohydrates, protein, and fat, can be gathered in winter and cooked in as many different ways as potatoes. They can also be dried, pulverized, and sifted to use as a flour substitute. Yellow cattail pollen is sweet and very nutritious. It can be used 1/2 and 1/2 with flour in any recipe calling for flour. Native Americans used cattail pollen to make mush.

GOLDEN BISCUITS
(Makes about 1 dozen)

>1 cup flour
>1 cup cattail pollen, cleaned (check for small yellow spiders)
>2 teaspoons baking powder
>1/2 teaspoon baking soda
>1/2 teaspoon salt
>4 tablespoons butter, melted
>3/4 cup yogurt

Mix dry ingredients together. Add butter and yogurt and mix well. Roll out dough onto a floured surface. Cut into biscuits and bake on a greased pan at 450° for 12 to 15 minutes or until done.

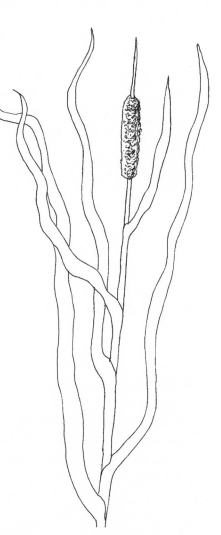

CEANOTHUS

Ceanothus spp.

Wild Lilac, California Lilac, Blue Blossom

Features: There are many varieties of ceanothus, ranging in size from small shrubs to small trees. Their fragrant flowers are usually pale lilac or white, but one rare variety has lilac-colored flowers which fade to white as they age. The variety pictured is densely branched. New branches are slender and green, but older branches and trunks are covered by a rough, grayish-brown bark. The small oval leaves have slightly toothed margins and grow irregularly spaced along branches. Panicles of lilac-colored flowers are borne on short stems along the branches.

Facts: Ceanothus bushes and trees can be found throughout the West except in low deserts. Their leaves can be gathered year-round and their flowers are available during spring and early summer. Some species of ceanothus contain saponins, soap-like substances that form lather when rubbed with water. Surprisingly, this only works for some people—other people just don't have the right chemistry. Native Americans had many uses for ceanothus. They gathered the seeds for food, used the flowers for soap, smoked the leaves, used the bark and roots for an astringent and tonic, and made a red dye from the roots.

Foods:
Tea: Put 6 to 8 small leaves and a few flowers into a cup. Add boiling water. Cover and steep for 10 minutes. This tea reputedly aids in the absorption of food and is good for the lymphatic system. A tea can also be made from the flowers. Both teas have a pleasant odor and a mild refreshing taste.

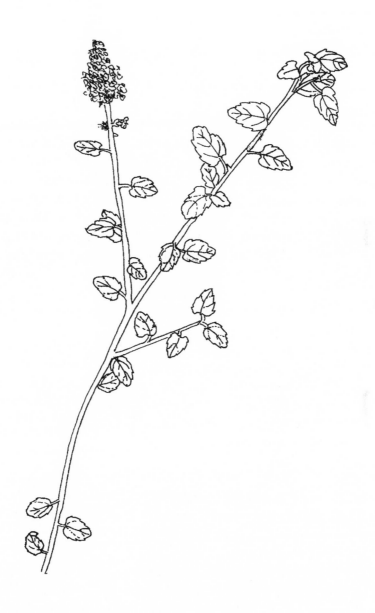

CHEESEWEED

Malva parviflora

Malva neglecta

Common Mallow, Cheese Mallow

Features: Cheeseweed is one of the first greens to appear in spring or after early rains. It grows everywhere. *M. parviflora* grows 1 to 3 feet tall, but *M. neglecta* grows only 5 to 8 inches tall. Both are annuals and they have slightly fuzzy, palmately-lobed leaves with 7 shallow lobes. The stems are located directly beneath the leaves at the point where all 7 main veins meet. The tiny white, pink or lavender flowers have 5 petals. Cheeseweed fruits, which grow at the junction of leaf stems and stalks, resemble miniature green cheeses.

Facts: Hardy cheeseweed can be found growing in waste places throughout the West. It is related to marshmallow, *Althea officinalis*, the original source of marshmallows. People used to use marshmallow's mucilaginous roots to make a soothing throat medicine. This tasted so good, after it was sweetened, that it became popular. Soon people were cooking marshmallow just because they enjoyed it. However, marshmallow roots are no longer included as an ingredient in the modern confection.

Foods:
Tea: Cooking liquid from cheeseweed leaves can be drunk as a mild tea. Another tea can be made by steeping several leaves with boiling water in a covered mug for 10 minutes.

Raw: In late winter or throughout spring, young leaves and shoots can be eaten as snacks or added to salads. Later on, from early spring until fall, the crisp and crunchy fruits, known as cheeses, can also be eaten raw. Cahuilla Indians ate the seeds.

Cooked: Young cheeseweed leaves can be steamed, boiled, sautéed, or added to soups and stews. They mix well with other ingredients, but are bland when cooked alone.

CHEESEWEED CALZONE
(Serves 3 – 4)

> Pizza or pie crust
> 1 cup cheeseweed greens, cleaned
> 1 clove garlic, minced
> 1/2 onion, diced
> 1 tablespoons olive oil
> 1 large tomato, diced
> 6 ounces ricotta
> 3 tablespoons Parmesan
> 3/4 cup grated mozzarella
> 1/4 cup sliced olives

Roll out a pizza or pie crust. Then steam the cheeseweed greens for 10 minutes. Drain and put them into a bowl. Then mix in the other ingredients. Place on 1/2 of the crust. Fold the crust over and press its edges together. Bake on a greased pan or cookie sheet at 425° for 20 minutes or until golden brown.

CHIA

Salvia columbariae

Features: There are several varieties of chia, some of which are on endangered plant lists. *S. columbariae* is a small annual that reaches a height of 3 to 24 inches. It has tiny, pale blue-violet flowers which grow in 1 to 3 whorls near the top of a slender, erect stem. Most of the leaves are basal, growing in a circle surrounding the stem. These dark green leaves are usually hairy and sometimes coarsely toothed. Be sure to check if your variety of chia is an endangered species before you harvest the seeds.

Facts: *Salvia columbariae* can be found growing in dry, open places throughout the West in spring. The seeds can be gathered from mature plants during summer. Chia was a very important seed plant for west coast Native Americans, who roasted or parched the seeds, ground them into flour, and then made mush from the flour or pressed it into cakes for later use. It is said that a brave could travel all day on a ration of 1 tablespoon of chia seeds. In addition, Native Americans utilized these seeds to help remove foreign matter from their eyes. Chia plants are also used in other countries around the world. The Cambodians and Mexicans both make a refreshing drink from a form of chia seeds.

Foods:
Raw: Tiny chia seeds can be eaten raw. If you hold them in your mouth before swallowing them, they become mucilaginous like gelatin. Some people think that they taste like watermelon seeds; whereas others find them tasteless. Do not, however, eat the chia seeds sold with "Chia Pets;" they may contain chemicals and be unsuitable for consumption.

Cooked: Chia seeds can be dried or roasted and then ground. The resulting meal can be eaten dry, diluted in a drink, or cooked with water to make a hot cereal.

CHIA COOLER
(Serves 1)

> 1 tablespoon chia seeds
> 1 cup water
> Lemon juice
> Sugar or honey

Soak the seeds for 15–20 minutes in water. Strain out the seeds, but retain the liquid. Flavor to taste with lemon juice, and sugar or honey. Drinks made from chia seeds are said to be thirst-quenching and energizing.

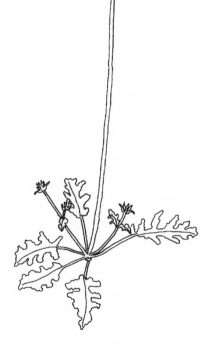

CHICKWEED

Stellaria media

Starwort

Features: Chickweed is a delightful late winter or early spring annual that grows up to 6 inches tall. At a time when most plants are still brown and shriveled, chickweed creates a glowing, apple-green carpet blanketing the ground. Its small, pointed, smooth-edged leaves grow alternately along the stalk on tiny individual leaf stems or directly attached. Tiny, white, star-like chickweed flowers have 4 to 5 deeply cleft petals.

Facts: Chickweed grows in a wide variety of habitats throughout the United States. The entire plant can be gathered from late winter until fall. It is one of the few greens to have a high copper content and is often mentioned as a diuretic or diet aid, although there is no concrete evidence of its effectiveness.

Foods:
Tea: Chickweed makes a pleasantly mild tea. First fill a cup 1/3 full with clean leaves and stems. Add boiling water. Cover and steep for 5 minutes. Strain and serve for a soothing hot drink.

Raw: The entire plant is good in salads and sandwiches, or just as a snack on the trail.

Cooked: Mild-flavored chickweed can be steamed, but this greatly reduces its volume and makes it relatively tasteless.

MAKRETZI SOUP
(Serves 2)

> 2 tablespoons butter
> 1 small onion, diced
> 2 cups chickweed, chopped
> 1/2 cup curly dock, chopped, (see page 42)
> 2 cups milk
> 1 potato, minced
> Dash paprika
> Salt and pepper to taste

Melt butter and sauté onion until clear. Stir in chickweed and curly dock and cook until wilted. Add more butter if necessary. Mix in the milk, potato and seasonings. Simmer until well blended for a delicious soup.

Recipe reprinted with permission from *Plant Lore of an Alaskan Island*, by Francis Kelso Graham, (Bothell, WA: Alaskan Northwest Books, 1985).

CHOKECHERRY

Prunus demissa

Features: Chokecherry is a large deciduous shrub or small tree that grows 3 to 25 feet tall. The dark green leaves are elliptical in shape, finely toothed along their edges, and grow alternately along branches. Sometimes the older leaves curl up along their spine, resembling tacos. Small white flowers grow along spikes only to be replaced by hanging clusters of abundant, shiny, red berries which are slightly larger than peas. These berries become almost black when mature. Chokecherry shrubs are very conspicuous after the berries appear during fall.

Facts: Chokecherry shrubs and trees grow in thickets in well-watered mountainous areas throughout the United States. The black, mature berries are available by September or October. Chockcherries can be eaten cooked when they are still red, or after they become black. Although the flesh of the berries is edible, their pits contain dangerous levels of cyanide. Children have died from eating only a few of these seeds. Toxic levels of cyanide have also been found in the leaves and inner bark of some species. The poison in the seeds can be neutralized by cooking. Native Americans leached the berries, ground them, and then boiled and ate them.

Foods:

USE WITH CAUTION.

Raw: If the pits are removed, the mature berries can be eaten raw, but they're very sour.

Cooked: Chokecherries make a delicious and colorful jam, jelly, syrup, or pie.

CHOKECHERRY JELLY
(Makes 1 1/2 pints)

      10 cups ripe chokecherries
      3 cups water
      3 cups sugar (approximately)
      1 package pectin
      1 teaspoon cinnamon
      Juice of 2 lemons

Clean the chokecherries and place them into a large pot. Mash them with a potato masher. Add water and stir. Bring to a boil, then cover and lower the heat. Simmer for 20 minutes, stirring constantly. Pour into a sieve lined with cheesecloth. Strain out the juice. Squeeze the remainder of juice from the cloth. Measure the juice and return it to the pot. Add 3 cups of sugar, (or an amount equal to the amount of juice), pectin, cinnamon, and lemon juice. Stir well. Heat to a rolling boil and continue boiling for 1 minute or until the mixture begins to thicken. Pour into sterilized containers and seal. It can also be frozen. Chokecherry jelly makes a great Christmas gift!

CHUFA

Cyperus esculentus

Nut Grass, Yellow Nut Grass

Features: Chufa is a 1 to 2 foot tall perennial sedge with a triangular stem. Pale green, grass-like leaves surround a slightly taller stalk. These leaves have a prominent midrib and they join with the stalk at its base. Another cluster of 8 to 9 smaller, ray-like leaves encircles the top of the stalk beneath its spikelets of flat, faded, straw-colored flowers. Most varieties of chufa produce small nutlike tubers from their roots.

Facts: Chufa grows in mud flats and marshy ground throughout the contiguous United States. The roots can be gathered from spring until fall. Since ancient times, people have consumed chufa tubers. They were eaten by Egyptians, and Spaniards used them to make a cold drink. Paiute Indians pounded the tubers together with tobacco leaves to make a remedy for athlete's foot.

Foods:
Raw: Mild-flavored young plants, their crisp, crunchy, root bases, and young tubers are all edible. Be sure that the water they're growing in or near is safe before you eat any chufa plants.

Cooked: The tubers can be cooked in all the different ways you cook potatoes.

CHUFA COOLER
(Makes 1 quart)

> 1/2 pound chufa tubers, cleaned
> 1 quart water
> Sugar to taste
> Vanilla (optional)

Soak chufa tubers in water for 2 days. Drain. Then crush them in 1 quart of water by hand, blender, or food processor. Strain and save the remaining liquid. Sweeten to taste. This creamy drink can also be used to make sherbet.

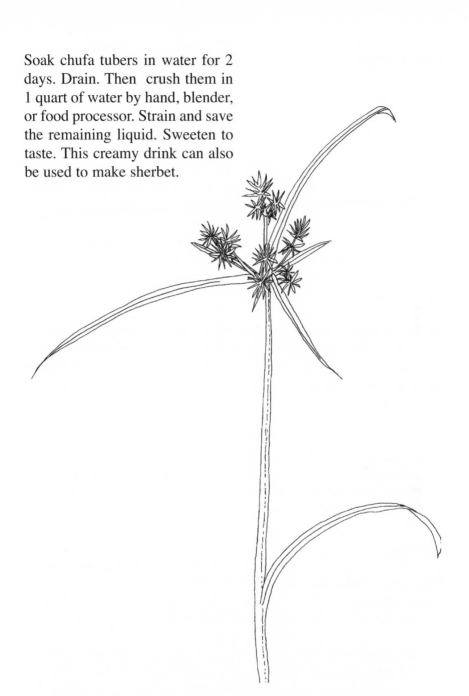

CLEAVERS

Galium aparine

Bedstraw

Features: Cleavers is a sparsely branched, sprawling, weak-stemmed vine that often climbs up other plants for support. Small, lance-shaped leaves grow in whorls of 4 to 8, and join directly to the stem. Tiny, star-shaped white flowers also grow from the stem at this point. After the flowers mature, they are replaced by small, dry, 2-lobed fruit resembling seedpods. The stems and leaves of cleavers are covered with tiny curved bristles that help them to cling to other plants.

Facts: *Galium aparine* grows in damp, shaded locations throughout the United States. It flowers in spring and the fruits can be gathered in early summer. Surprisingly, this unobtrusive plant has many uses. As one of its names implies, bedstraw was often used to stuff mattresses. In addition, a salve can be made from cleavers to soothe burns and help heal skin sores, a sieve can be fashioned from its vines, and it can be used to coagulate milk and make cheese because it contains rennet. Since it is remotely related to coffee, the minute fruits can be used to make a coffee-like brew. However, because it contains no caffeine, diehard coffee drinkers may find the results disappointing.

Foods:
Tea: For a truly tasty tea, put a few pieces of flowering cleavers into a cup. Add boiling water. Cover and steep for 5 to 10 minutes. Strain and serve. Cleavers tea is often recommended for weight loss because of its reputed diuretic properties.

Cooked: Before flowering, the stems can be cooked and eaten hot or cold for a salad. When gathered in early summer, tiny cleavers fruits can be roasted and ground to make a coffee-like beverage.

CLEAVERS "COFFEE"
(Makes 4 cups)

> 4 - 8 tablespoons cleavers fruits, cleaned
> 4 cups water

Lightly roast the fruits in a low oven until brown (some people prefer light golden brown whereas others prefer dark brown). Grind them in a coffee mill or blender. Prepare these grounds the same way you would normally prepare coffee grounds, except you may want to use more per cup because the flavor is milder.

CLOVER

Trifolium spp.

Features: Clovers are small herbs which can grow as tall as 16 inches, but are usually much shorter. Their green, trifoliate leaves are sometimes decorated with a pale green V-shaped design. The white disc flowers of *T. repens* and the pink or red disc flowers of *T. pratense* form dense, spherical, flower heads. Each flowerhead and each leaf is on a separate stem. These stems join together at their base.

Slightly branched sweet clover *(Melilotus spp.)* also has trifoliate clover-like leaves, but is taller than the trifoliums. Its leaves are a darker shade of green and its disc flowers, which are yellow (*M. indicus*) or white (*M. albus*), do not form spheres. Instead, they grow along flower spikes, and the leaves grow along stalks and branches. Although some species of clover are annuals, the two species covered here are perennials.

Facts: Clover grows best in meadows and similar moist locations in most of the United States including Alaska. It tastes best when gathered in spring or summer. All parts of clover are edible and high in plant protein but raw clover is difficult for people to digest unless it is soaked for 2 or 3 hours in salt water. Sweet clover, in particular, should be eaten sparingly. Native Americans ate clover raw or steamed, sometimes drying the steamed plants and saving them for winter use. Clover also has medicinal uses. Red clover is considered an antispasmodic and an aid in cases of indigestion.

Foods:

USE IN MODERATION.

Tea: Put 1 teaspoon of dried clover blossoms into a cup. Fill with boiling water. Cover and steep for 10 minutes. Strain and sweeten to taste. This mild tea is said to be a soothing tonic for sore throats and coughs.

Raw: Fresh flowers can be eaten as a snack or added to salads. To make them easier to digest, some people prefer to soak them first.

Cooked: The roots can be cooked, but they're very small. First clean and chop them into 1/2-inch pieces. Then boil them for 5 minutes. Drain, season and serve with butter. Clover blossoms can be added to pancake batter.

Dried: Clover blossoms can be dried and added to bread.

POTATOES WITH CLOVER
(Serves 3 – 4)

2 cups water
4 potatoes, diced
1 cup clover leaves, chopped
2 tablespoons butter
1 onion, minced
2 cloves garlic, minced
Salt and pepper

Boil water. Add potatoes and clover leaves. Cook until potatoes are tender. Meanwhile, melt butter and sauté onion and garlic until the onion is soft. Drain potatoes and clover leaves and add to the onion mixture. Season with salt and pepper.

COTTONWOOD

Populus fremontii

Fremont Cottonwood

Features: Cottonwoods are tall deciduous trees that can reach heights of 60 feet. Growing on long, slender stems, cottonwood leaves always seem to be in motion. The slightest breeze will set them to shimmering and dancing in the sunlight. Young cottonwoods have smooth gray bark which later becomes rough and brown. On older trees, branching usually begins about 5 or 6 feet above the ground. New branches are slender and flexible. Shiny, green, spade-shaped leaves turn yellow in autumn, often becoming spotted with brown before they fall off. Tiny flowers grow in spike-like masses known as catkins.

Facts: Cottonwoods favor stream beds and other moist locations throughout the United States and Canada. Leaf buds are available from early spring through fall and sometimes during winter, but the best time to gather them is spring. Since terminal buds are also the new growth of the branches, it is important not to pick all the buds off any one area of a tree. Cottonwoods contain aspirin-like compounds that reduce pain, fever, and inflammation. They also make good summer fires because they give light without much heat. These trees were used by Native Americans to make wooden mortars for grinding soft foods such as mesquite. Hopis carve Kachina dolls from the roots.

Foods:
Tea: Start with 1 cottonwood leaf and place it in a cup. Add boiling water. Cover and steep for 5 to 10 minutes. Because cottonwood tea is similar to aspirin, it is important not to make it any stronger than necessary. Strength depends upon the quality of the leaves, the number used, and the length of time they are steeped. This slightly bitter tea is said to cure headaches and minor pains, but it shouldn't be used with anticoagulants or by people who are allergic to aspirin.

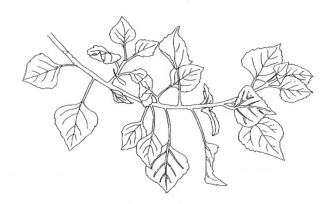

Raw: The cambium, or inner layer of bark, is a nourishing food source in spring. Because removal of inner bark is harmful to trees, it should only be eaten as a last resort. Cottonwood catkins can also be eaten raw.

Cooked: The cambium can be boiled or ground and used as a flour substitute in times of great need. Cottonwood catkins can be added to stews.

Dried: Cottonwood leaf buds can be used fresh or dried to make a soothing ointment for burns and skin irritations.

COTTONWOOD SALVE
(Makes 1 pint)

> 1 cup cottonwood leaf buds (the more aromatic the better)
> 1 wide-mouthed pint jar
> 1 cup extra virgin olive oil
> 1 sheet of beeswax (18 inches square)

Clean the buds and put them into a jar. Add olive oil. Cover with paper towel and leave in a warm location for 1 week. Strain the liquid into a pot and heat on medium. Add beeswax to the warm oil. Stirring occasionally, continue heating until wax is melted. Pour the mixture into the jar. The salve will solidify as it cools. For a softer salve, add less beeswax. Cover tightly.

CREOSOTE

Larrea tridentata

Chaparral

Features: Creosote is a prolific, bushy shrub of southwestern deserts. After a rain you can smell its pleasantly pungent odor from far away. *Larrea tridentata* can grow up to 12 feet high, but usually is much shorter. Its brittle, reddish-brown trunks, which later turn gray, grow from a central point on the ground—growing outward and upward as they branch out. Tiny, shiny, pointed, yellow-green leaves grow in clusters on minute stems along the branches. These leaves are often sticky, especially after a rain. Small, bright yellow creosote flowers appear in spring, followed by round, gray, fuzzy fruits which are slightly smaller than peas.

Facts: Creosote grows in desert areas throughout the southwestern United States. Most people gather sprigs of leaves and flowers in spring, but they can be collected throughout the year. Creosote leaves contain 16% plant protein, and have antiseptic properties. The Cahuilla Indians made solutions and poultices from creosote to use on open wounds—a treatment that helped to draw out poisons and prevent infections. They also used creosote tea to combat allergies. Even today, many people find that creosote tea relieves colds, flu symptoms, and upset stomachs. Research shows that creosote contains a material known as nordihydroguaiaretic acid which delays fats from turning rancid.

Foods:

USE IN MODERATION.

Tea: Put a small sprig of leaves into a cup. Add boiling water. Cover and steep for 5 to 10 minutes—depending on the desired strength. Strain and serve. Save the sprig. It can be reused once or twice more. This tea has a strong but very pleasant flavor. You may want to sweeten it. Creosote tea is said to be a general tonic, good for; coughs, colds, chest infections, bowel complaints, stomach cramps, and congestion. It is even reputed to be effective in curing cancer. However, a Cahuilla Indian advised me not to drink this tea more often than 3 times a week because creosote is so potent. It is not recommended to drink this tea while taking other medication.

Cooked: Creosote leaves can be boiled and the steam inhaled to relieve congestion. Solutions and poultices can be made from the heated leaves to help heal open wounds and prevent infection.

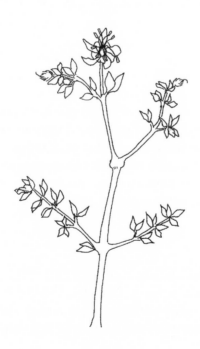

CURLY DOCK

Rumex crispus

Dock, Sour Dock, Curled Dock, Yellow Dock

Features: Curly dock is a tall conspicuous plant. Young plants consist of clusters of upright lanceolate leaves which are 3 to 10 inches long with curled margins. Each leaf grows on its own stout stem, with the stems meeting at ground level. A woody flower stalk, which can grow over 5 feet tall, rises from the center of the leaf cluster. Additional leaves, growing along the stalk and branches, become progressively smaller as they approach the tips. Densely packed, whorled clusters of inconspicuous flowers grow in tiers along the branches and at their tips, followed by numerous tiny seeds encased in small, green, triangular, paper-like sheaths. Curly dock changes color as it ages, becoming yellow, gold, rusty brown, or red.

Facts: *Rumex crispus* grows in waste places and fields throughout the United States and is available during most of the year. It contains oxalic acid which gives it a sour flavor. Although moderate amounts of oxalic acid are not harmful, large quantities may cause stomach upsets. Oxalic acid crystals can accumulate in your body. Some references state that cooking or freezing curly dock breaks down the acid and neutralizes its effect; others say that it requires protein to neutralize it. To be safe, eat curly dock in moderation and combine it with protein. Curly dock is high in vitamin C.

Foods:
Tea: Tear up a small, young leaf and put it into a cup. Add boiling water, cover and steep for 5 minutes. Strain, sweeten and serve. Although tea brewed from the roots is said to be mildly laxative, tea made from the leaves does not appear to have any medicinal uses.

Raw: Young leaves, often available year-round, especially in spring and fall, can be eaten as snacks or added to salads.

Cooked: They can be boiled, steamed, or stir-fried. Curly dock leaves have a lemon-like flavor and are very tasty when used in moderation.

DIANE'S FRENCH SOUR SOUP
(Serves 4-6)

> 1 tablespoon butter
> 1 cup new curly dock greens, chopped
> 1 tablespoon butter
> 1 onion, diced
> 4 potatoes, cubed
> 3 cups water or broth
> 2 cups milk
> 1/2 cup sour cream
> Salt and pepper

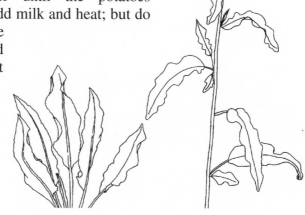

In a large pot melt 1 tablespoon butter and sauté greens until limp. Set them aside. Then melt the other tablespoon of butter and sauté onion until clear. Return the greens to the pot; add potatoes and water or broth and cover. Bring to a boil. Lower heat and simmer until the potatoes become tender. Add milk and heat; but do not boil. Stir in the sour cream and season with salt and pepper.

CURRANT

Ribes cereum

Wild Currant, Squaw Currant

Features: Currant shrubs are short, growing from 3 to 4 feet high. Their small, coarse leaves have 3 slightly distinct lobes and grow alternately along branches. The pea-sized currants of *Ribes cereum* are round and green, becoming deep red when ripe. These are the tastiest of the currant berries. Sierra currant, Ribes nevadense, grows at higher elevations. Its leaves are larger and more deeply lobed, and its berries, which grow in hanging clusters, become blue-black when ripe. Gooseberry bushes, *Ribes speciosum,* also members of the currant family, have slightly larger berries which are covered with prickles. Mature gooseberries are either red or green, depending on the variety.

Facts: Currant shrubs grow in moist places throughout the United States. Ripe currants are ready to pick during summer. Native Americans often used currants to make pemmican. First they dried the berries, and then pounded them together with meat and fat. Currants are high in vitamin C, phosphorus and iron.

Foods:
Raw: Currants can be eaten right off the bush or added to fruit salads after the seeds are removed. All currants are edible, but not all are equally sweet.

Cooked: The leaves are reputed to be edible, but I have yet to find a palatable recipe. If you want to try cooking some, be sure to pick young leaves before flowers and fruit appear. Currants can be made into jams, jellies, and pies.

Dried: They can also be dried for future use.

CURRANT FRUIT LEATHER
(Approximately 8 strips)

> 4 cups currants, cleaned
> 1 cup water
> 1 cup sugar or 1/2 cup honey

Heat berries and water together on medium heat until currants are soft. Strain out seeds and save juice. Add sugar or honey and blend well. Put plastic wrap on a cookie sheet and spread puréed fruit on the sheet. Heat slowly in the sun, an oven, or a dehydrator until firm but not brittle. Eat immediately or roll and store in an airtight container. The number of pieces this recipe yields varies according to the size and thickness of each piece.

CURRANT PANCAKES
(Serves 2)

> 2 cups flour
> 1 2/3 cups milk
> 2 eggs
> 1/2 cup apple juice concentrate
> 1/2 cup currants, cleaned and seeded
> 1/8 tsp salt
> 1/4 teaspoon vanilla
> Butter

Mix all the ingredients together except butter. Melt 1 pat of butter in a hot pan or on a grill. Drop spoonfuls of batter onto the grill and brown the pancakes on both sides. Add more butter as needed.

DANDELION

Taraxacum officinale

Features: Everyone recognizes the sunny yellow flowers of perennial dandelion. Usually referred to as weeds, dandelions are highly nutritious. Appearing first as a rosette, dandelion leaves are lanceolate-shaped with pointed lobes and irregularly toothed margins. Each leaf grows on a separate stem and all the stems grow from a single, central taproot. Weak flower stems grow up from among the leaves and reach 2 to 12 inches in height. Each flower stem is topped by a single dandelion blossom.

Facts: Dandelions are found throughout North America and Europe in moist locations. Their flowers are most evident from late winter through autumn. Dandelion roots are best when collected from spring until fall, but the leaves are most tender from late winter through early spring. These leaves should be gathered while they are young and tender because older leaves are bitter. In colder climates, dandelion leaves are a welcome green after a winter of preserved foods. This is one of the first plants to appear in spring and is often used as a "spring tonic," or just enjoyed as a fresh green. Dandelions are rich in vitamins A, B and C. Their name derives from the French *dent de lion,* which means "Lion's tooth."

Foods:
Tea: Put 2 teaspoons of freshly chopped greens into a cup. Add boiling water. Cover and steep for 5 minutes for a mild tea or 8 hours for a cold remedy. Strain, sweeten and serve.

Raw: In spring, very young leaves and crowns can be eaten raw or added to salads. Older leaves are too bitter to be eaten uncooked.

Cooked: Young leaves need to be steamed or boiled for 10 to 20 minutes. If the leaves are old and bitter, use 2 changes of water. They can also be stir-fried or added to soups. Dandelion roots can be steamed, boiled, and baked; or dried, ground, and used as a coffee substitute. The flowers can be added to cakes and pancakes to flavor and lighten the batter.

POTATO AND DANDELION SALAD
(Serves 2)

> 1 potato, cooked and sliced thin
> 1/2 cup young dandelion greens, torn
> Vinaigrette dressing (see page 77)
> Dill, fresh or dried

Combine all ingredients and serve.

DANDELION AND EGG SALAD
(Serves 2)

> 2 hard-boiled eggs
> 1/2 cup young dandelion greens, torn
> Mayonnaise

Toss all the ingredients together and serve or use in a sandwich.

ELDERBERRY

Sambucus caerulea

Features: Elderberries are large shrubs or small trees 6 to 15 feet tall. Their leaves are compound with 5 to 7 leaflets. Before small dense umbels of aromatic white flowers appear, elderberry trees are relatively inconspicuous. When their flowers bloom in spring, these trees seem to be everywhere. Eventually the flowers are replaced by clusters of small greenish-white berries that become bluish-gray dusted with powdery-white when mature. Then these trees do a vanishing act. Birds eat the berries, the leaves dry up and drop off, and the showy elderberry fades into the background.

Facts: Elderberries are found growing in rich moist soil throughout the United States. Native Americans often called the elderberry, "The Tree of Music," because they made flutes from its branches. First they removed the soft pith, and then carved holes for different notes. Cases of poisoning from some elderberry flutes have been reported. Mature blue or black elderberries are edible when cooked; however, the raw berries, leaves, and bark of edible varieties have been known to have laxative effects, and the red berries of the red elderberry *(Sambucus microbotrys)* are poisonous! Fortunately, this species grows at 9,000 to 10,000 feet, so you are unlikely to confuse it with the others.

Foods:

USE WITH CAUTION.

Tea: Put fresh or dried flowers into a cup. Add boiling water. Cover and steep for 10 minutes. The resulting aromatic tea is pleasantly mild and a reputed cure for: colds, constipation, rheumatic complaints and nervous disorders.

Raw: Some people find the raw berries laxative in nature. The berries of the red elder, which does not grow here, have poisonous seeds. It's always safest to cook elderberries before eating them.

Cooked: Cooked elderberries can be made into delicious jams, jellies and wine. The flowers, called "elderblow," can be used in many tasty recipes. They can be added to pancakes, waffles, muffins, or cakes; to lighten and sweeten the batter. They can also be dipped in batter and fried.

ELDERBERRY JAM
(Makes 1 1/2 pints)

> 3 pounds ripe elderberries
> Juice from 1 lemon
> 1 package pectin
> 3 cups sugar

Mash the berries and simmer them for 15 minutes, stirring occasionally. Strain them using cheesecloth. Combine the resulting liquid, lemon juice, and pectin. Bring to a boil for 1 minute, stirring constantly. Add sugar. Bring to a rolling boil and boil for 2 minutes more while continuing to stir. Pour into sterilized containers and seal. Store or freeze for future use.

EPHEDRA

Ephedra spp.

Desert Tea, Mormon Tea, Squaw Tea, Joint Fir

Features: Ephedra is a brittle, perennial desert shrub that grows 1 to 4 feet tall. Its slender branches appear to be jointed, growing opposite each other or in clusters. Miniture, inconspicuous, scale-like leaves grow in pairs along the branches and later fall off. The new growth, which appears in spring, is pale green with tiny yellow flowers growing along the branches. These branches gradually turn brown with the bases of older bushes becoming woody. There are 7 different species of ephedra in California alone.

Facts: Morman tea grows in warm, arid regions throughout the western states and usually blooms from April until May. It can be gathered during any season and is good either fresh or dried. All species of ephedra make good tea. Over the years, ephedra has been known for its medicinal properties. The Chinese use a stronger variety of ephedra as a general tonic. Settlers, Spaniards, and Native Americans used ephedra as: a tonic, a blood purifier, a diuretic, and an aid for kidney troubles and weak lungs. The Cahuilla Indians made a strong tea by selecting twigs that have a red streak running through the center and boiling them for 30 minutes—until the liquid became dark red. They harvested these twigs from June through November. Because of its medicinal properties, this tea should be drunk in moderation, especially the Chinese variety. Ephedra twigs and leaves were also boiled to make a light brown dye.

Foods:

USE WITH CAUTION.

Tea: Put several green or brown twigs into a cup. Add boiling water. Cover and steep for 20 minutes. Remove the twigs, but don't throw them away. They can be used once or twice more. People who are sensitive to caffeine should not drink this tea.

Raw: It is said that ephedra twigs can be chewed to relieve thirst and that they have a mildly pleasant flavor.

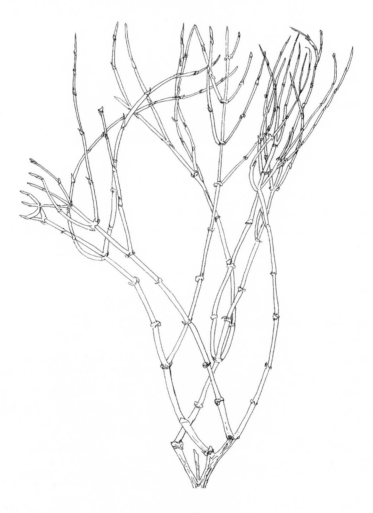

EUCALYPTUS

Eucalyptus globulus

Blue Gum Tree, Gum Tree

Features: There are hundreds of species of eucalyptus trees. Most are tall and majestic. The blue gum is characterized by its shaggy bark which hangs in strips, becoming a real fire hazard. This attractive bark has strips and patches that are different shades of brown, gray, and white. Dark green eucalyptus leaves are usually lance or sickle-shaped with smooth margins. They hang in orderly rows from the branches. Young leaves are silvery-blue above, green beneath, and somewhat rounder in shape than older leaves. Small, white, petalless flowers, which display numerous stamens, mature into grayish-blue, angular nuts about the size of gumballs.

Facts: Eucalyptus trees are not native to the Southwest but do well there. Fast-growing evergreen trees, they were originally imported from Australia in 1856 to provide a ready supply of wood for railroad ties. Unfortunately, this wood proved to be too soft to use. Eucalyptus leaves and nuts contain a disinfectant which is said to repel fleas. They make attractive flea collars when strung alternately with small, brightly colored beads, and have been proven to be effective for several months at a time when worn by dogs and cats.

Foods:

USE IN MODERATION.

Tea: Younger, rounder, more aromatic leaves are the best to use for tea. Put 1/2 of a leaf into a cup. Fill with boiling water. Cover and steep for 10 minutes. Strain and sweeten. Eucalyptus tea is said to be an antidote for colds, flu, fevers, and sinus infections. The steam is also good for colds and sinus infections.

WARNING: Although sulfur shelf mushrooms are generally edible, those growing on eucalyptus trees are not!

FIDDLEHEAD

Pteridium aquilinum

Bracken Fern, Pasture Brake

Features: The young curled fronds of bracken ferns, called "fiddleheads," are covered with silvery fuzz. First appearing during early spring and continuing until midsummer, they reach heights of 2 to 6 feet.

Facts: Bracken ferns grow along streams and in other moist locations throughout the United States. The fiddleheads are edible, but only if they are under 6 to 8 inches tall and if they are still curled. Once the leaves begin to uncurl, it's too late; even if the plant is less than 8 inches high. This is because fiddleheads prefer to grow in soil that is rich in selenium—a cumulative poison. All parts of these fiddleheads contain some selenium, the larger, more mature ferns contain the most. Excessive amounts of selenium have been found to be harmful to humans. For this reason, fiddleheads should be gathered in spring while they are young. Fiddlehead roots contain a lot of sodium. Ashes from the cooked roots can be used as a salt substitute.

Foods:

USE WITH CAUTION.

Before cooking, remove fuzz from fiddleheads. This can be done by simply passing them through your fingers.

Cooked: Tie a bunch of cleaned fiddleheads together and steam them in an upright position in a covered pot. Cook for about 30 minutes, or until tender. Drain well and season with salt and pepper. Butter, lemon butter, or sauce can be added. Fiddleheads can also be stir-fried. They look and taste a bit like asparagus.

FIDDLEHEADS WITH SAUCE BÉCHAMEL

(Serves 4)

1 tablespoon butter
2 tablespoons flour
1 cup milk
2 tablespoons Parmesan (optional)
Salt and pepper

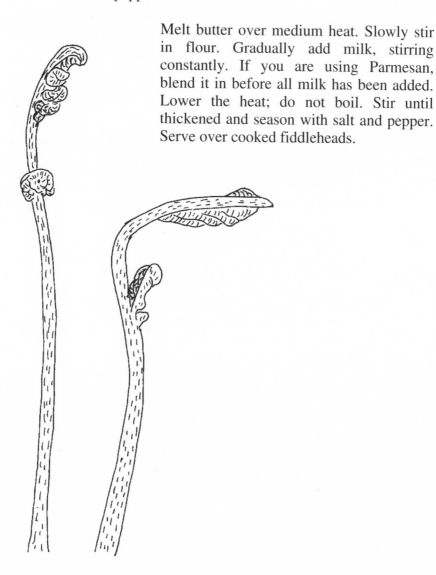

Melt butter over medium heat. Slowly stir in flour. Gradually add milk, stirring constantly. If you are using Parmesan, blend it in before all milk has been added. Lower the heat; do not boil. Stir until thickened and season with salt and pepper. Serve over cooked fiddleheads.

GLASSWORT

Salicornia subterminalis

Pickle Plant

Features: Glasswort is a short, perennial succulent with jointed stems, and usually grows under 1 foot tall. Its leafless branches are also jointed, and grow opposite each other in alternating pairs. These branches are shorter than the stem, and curve upward, forming a U-shape with the stem. Young plants are celery green, often turning red as they age. Older glasswort stems become woody. All parts of glasswort taste salty because it grows in moist, alkaline locations.

Facts: Glasswort grows in western coastal salt marshes from Mexico to Canada, in Europe and in Asia. During spring, the entire plant can be eaten. Later, only the tender tips are tasty. From June until October, Cahuillas and other Native Americans gathered the seeds and ground them into meal. Because the ashes of burned glasswort are rich in sodium, they were once used to manufacture glass and a soap called "barilla."

Foods:

Raw: Glasswort can be eaten raw. It's salty, moist, and crunchy, and mixes well with other vegetables.

Cooked: Chopped glasswort can be added to omelets and stir-fries, but glasswort is most often used to make pickles. Don't forget to taste before adding salt.

GLASSWORT PICKLES
(Makes about 1 quart)

> 1 quart vinegar
> 1/2 cup sugar
> 2 tablespoons pickling spices
> 2 bay leaves
> 1 small onion, chopped
> 4 cups young glasswort stems

Boil all the ingredients together, except the glasswort. For crunchy pickles put the fresh stems into several jars. (For softer pickles, boil or steam the stems for 3 to 5 minutes before placing them into the jars.) Then pour the boiled liquid over the stems, completely covering them, and almost to the top of the jars. Seal the jars and let them stand for 1 month before using.

GOLDENROD

Solidago californica

Features: *Solidago californica* is a hardy perennial herb that decorates both dry and sandy open areas and woodlands with its sunny yellow flowers throughout summer. Goldenrod blossoms are a welcome contrast to the dull, dried plants of this season. California goldenrod grows in clusters of stiff erect stems, which reach 2 to 4 feet in height. The numerous narrow oval-shaped leaves come to a point at the tip. Each leaf is on a tiny stem and the leaves at the base of a plant are larger than those farther up. The margins of these leaves can be either smooth or slightly toothed. Pleasantly pungent golden flowers, each on a separate stem, cluster closely together along the top of flower stems, often resembling a Mohawk haircut. The flowers are mostly ray flowers with some disk flowers mixed in. There are about 60 different varieties of goldenrod. *S. californica* resembles *Solidago odora,* the common sweet goldenrod of New England. Goldenrod is sometimes confused with goldenbush (*Haplopappus*) because both plants grow in dry, sunny locations, and they resemble each other. However, goldenbush appears earlier during the year, the leaves are more obviously serrated, it is usually a taller plant, and the flowers are not as densely clustered.

Facts: Goldenrod grows throughout the United States. Its flowers can be gathered during summer, but the stems and leaves are best collected from summer until fall. Early settlers dried it and used it for tea and food. Native Americans sprinkled the dry powdered leaves on wounds. They also used a tea made from dried leaves and flowers to relieve kidney problems and prevent gas. Liquid from boiled stems and leaves was used to wash hair, prevent hair loss, and add highlights to blond hair.

Foods:

Tea: Put 6 dried leaves or 3 small, dried flower stems into a cup. Add boiling water. Cover and steep for 10 to 20 minutes for a pleasantly mild tea. The flowers produce a sweeter tea than the leaves.

Cooked: Goldenrod flowers can be added to pancakes, biscuits, muffins, and cookies to lighten the batter. The greens are also edible and can be cooked as a potherb or added to soups to thicken them.

DESSERT CREPES
(Serves 2)

> 3/4 cup flour
> 1/3 cup goldenrod flowers, chopped
> 1 cup milk
> 2 eggs, beaten
> 1/2 teaspoon salt
> 1/2 cup sugar
> 1 teaspoon butter, melted
> 1 apple, grated
> Additional butter

Combine all ingredients except the apple. Beat until smooth. Add the apple. Melt additional butter in a frying pan. Brown the crepes on both sides. Serve immediately or keep them warm in the oven.

HOOKER'S EVENING PRIMROSE

Oenothera hookeri

Features: Attractive hooker's evening primrose usually grows 1 1/2 to 4 feet high and is adorned with small clusters of large, showy, bright yellow, 4-petaled flowers that close during the heat of the day and open up again at dusk. If you're patient, you can often hear a snap when they open. This lovely plant grows in two stages. First-year plants are ground-hugging rosettes of flat, fuzzy, lance-shaped leaves 4 to 8 inches long. Flower stalks don't appear until the second year.

Facts: Hooker's evening primrose grows near rivers or in other moist places throughout the United States. The roots should only be gathered from first-year plants, especially if they are to be cooked. The best time to gather them is from late fall until early spring. Tea made from the dried roots is sometimes used to relieve pain caused by menstrual cramps. Research is being conducted to see if the roots or seeds can help control multiple sclerosis or other degenerative diseases. The seeds contain gamma-linoleic acid.

Foods:
Tea: Liquid left over from cooked evening primrose roots or leaves can be used as tea. However, it tends to be bitter and tastes better when sweetened. This tea is reputed to be somewhat diuretic, laxative, and sedative in nature. Some people drink it as a kidney remedy.

Raw: In early spring, leaves from young plants can be eaten in salads. Young shoots can also be eaten raw, but they tend to be bitter.

Cooked: First-year leaves are good when steamed or boiled for 5-10 minutes. If they are bitter, they may need to be boiled twice. They taste better if you add butter flavored with orange or lemon juice. Young roots can also be boiled and eaten. Peel and slice them crosswise before cooking.

PRIMROSE-LENTIL SOUP
(Serves 4 – 6)

    1 1/2 tablespoons olive oil
    1 small onion, chopped
    1 clove garlic, minced
    2 stalks celery, sliced
    1/2 cup lentils
    5 cups broth or water
    1 cup carrots, sliced
    1 cup first-year evening primrose leaves, chopped
    Salt and pepper
    Cumin (about 1 teaspoon)

Heat olive oil and sauté onion and garlic until clear. Stir in celery and heat for 2 more minutes. Add lentils and broth or water. Cover.

Bring soup to a boil, lower heat, and simmer until lentils are tender—about 45 minutes. Add carrots and cook 5 minutes more at medium heat. Then stir in primrose leaves and cook until tender— about 5 to 10 minutes more. Season with salt and pepper. Add cumin to taste.

LAMB'S QUARTERS

Chenopodium album

Goosefoot, Wild Spinach

Features: *Chenopodium album* is officially recognized by Philip Munz in *A Flora of Southern California* as "Lamb's Quarters." Not only do people call most members of the Chenopodium family "lamb's quarters," but some also call them "pigweed," a name which is usually applied to amaranth. A prolific annual plant, lamb's quarters can grow up to 10 feet tall! Green, goosefoot-shaped leaves with pale undersides grow alternately along strong, 5-sided stems and branches. New terminal leaves form clusters, and their central leaves appear to be dusted with white or pale lavender powder. Drooping clusters of inconspicuous green flowers, growing at the intersection of branches and stems, develop into numerous tiny black seeds. Often the stems and branches of *C. album* have vertical burgundy stripes.

Facts: Lamb's quarters grow almost everywhere throughout the United States. All members of the Chenopodium family are edible. Mild and tender, lamb's quarters are very popular and can be used in any recipe calling for raw or cooked greens. They resemble spinach in flavor and contain vitamin C, iron, and potassium.

Foods:
Raw: In spring and summer, young leaves and tender shoots can be eaten in salads and sandwiches. In summer and fall, seeds can be gathered and sprouted.

Cooked: All parts of young plants can be steamed, boiled, or sautéed. Older plants tend to become tough, although the new growth at the tips of the branches may still be still tender.

Dried: The seeds can be dried, ground, and used for mush or bread.

LAMB'S QUARTERS PARMESAN
(Serves 4)

> 4 medium potatoes, thinly sliced
> 1 cup water
> 3 tablespoons butter
> 1 onion, sliced
> 4 cups lamb's quarters, cleaned
> 1 cup milk
> 6 tablespoons Parmesan
> 2 eggs
> 2 tablespoons flour
> 1 teaspoon salt
> 1/4 teaspoon pepper

Boil potatoes in water for 10 minutes. Remove them from the liquid, saving both. Melt butter and sauté onion until clear. Stir in greens and reserved potato water. Cover and cook for 5 minutes. Meanwhile, mix together: milk, 3 tablespoons Parmesan, eggs, flour, salt and pepper. Spread out 1/2 of the potatoes in a glass baking dish, cover with lamb's quarters and onions, and then layer the rest of the potatoes. Pour the milk mixture over everything. Sprinkle with remaining Parmesan. Bake at 350° for 30 minutes or until done. This dish goes well with tossed green salad.

LAMB'S QUARTERS, #2

Chenopodium fremontii

Features: *Chenopodium fremontii,* an annual, is one of the many edible plants inappropriately called "lamb's quarters." A close relative to *C. album*, it has the distinctive 5-sided stem and numerous branches, but its leaves are smaller and more evenly toothed than the official lamb's quarters. It's a shorter plant, only growing 8 to 48 inches high, and sometimes its older stems turn a rich burgundy color. People often call amaranth (*Amaranthus retroflexus*) lamb's quarters, too. This can create confusion unless you refer to their Latin names. Fortunately, both plants are edible and quite similar in flavor.

Facts: *Chenopodium fremontii* can be found in diverse habitats throughout the United States. Its leaves and shoots are best gathered over spring and summer, but the seeds should be collected during summer and fall.

Foods:
Raw: This "lamb's quarters" can also be eaten raw. It's good as a trail snack or added to salads and sandwiches.

Cooked: Young leaves and stems are good boiled, steamed, stir-fried or sautéed. They're very mild and mix well with stronger-flavored greens such as mustard. Small, nutritious lamb's quarters seeds can be roasted and ground to use in bread or mush.

INCREDIBLE GREEN PIZZA
(Makes 2 10-inch pizzas)

    2 pizza crusts
    8 ounces tomato sauce
    3 ounces tomato paste
    1 teaspoon basil, dried or fresh

1/2 teaspoon salt
Pinch sugar
1/4 teaspoon thyme
1/4 teaspoon oregano
1/2 cup water
1 1/2 cups fresh lamb's quarters, cleaned
1 cup pepperoni (optional)
1 cup mozzarella, grated

Place the pizza crusts onto greased pans. Mix all the sauce ingredients together and heat on low, stirring constantly. When it's heated, spread the sauce over the pizza crusts. Meanwhile, boil about 1 inch of water in a pot. Add lamb's quarters to the boiling water. Cover and steam for 3 minutes. Drain the greens well, and then spread them over the sauce. If you are using pepperoni, add it next. Sprinkle with grated cheese. Bake at 350° for 20 to 30 minutes or until done.

LEMONADEBERRY
Rhus integrifolia

SQUAW BUSH
R. trilobata

SUGAR BUSH
R. ovata

Features: These three members of the Rhus family are grouped together because they are often confused, and because they are all prepared the same way. Lemonadeberry and sugar bush are the most similar. They're both evergreen shrubs with leathery oval leaves, but lemonadeberry leaves are smaller, flatter, and have rounded ends. Sugar bush leaves fold along the middle like tacos, and have pointed tips. All three of these bushes have clusters of small, flat, sticky red berries. Lemonadeberry has the largest berries, and sugar bush has the smallest. Sugar bush berries are covered with a sweet, sticky, white coating. Lemonadeberry grows 3 to 10 feet high, sugar bush grows 5 to 15 feet high, and squaw bush only grows up to 5 feet in height. Squaw bush, a deciduous shrub, is often confused with poison oak because they both have leaves comprised of 3 leaflets. However, all of squaw bush's leaflets meet at a central point, whereas only 2 of poison oak's leaflets meet, and poison oak's central leaflet is on a short, extended stem (see page 192).

Facts: All three of these bushes grow in chaparral brush and oak woodlands throughout the Southwest. Lemonadeberries are available from late spring through early summer, but sugar bush berries mature a little later. Squaw bush berries do not ripen until midsummer. Squaw bush is also known as basket bush because Native Americans used its young flexible shoots for making baskets. Sometimes they purposely burned down old plants in order to have a fresh supply of new shoots in spring. Each shoot was divided into three long pieces which were coiled and set aside to dry until needed for baskets. Then they were soaked until they became flexible again.

Foods:

Raw: All of these berries have a sour, refreshing flavor and can be sucked on or made into a pleasant drink when they are ripe and sugar is added. Because they contain large seeds, it's not advisable to swallow them.

ALMOST LEMONADE
(Makes 2 quarts)

> 1/2 cup berries, cleaned
> 2 quarts water
> About 1 cup sugar

Soak the berries in water for 1/2 hour. Strain them out and sweeten the remaining liquid to taste. Don't let the clear color fool you—this drink definitely has a lemon-like flavor!

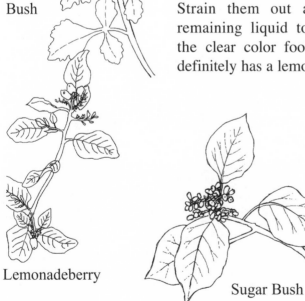

Squaw Bush

Lemonadeberry

Sugar Bush

LONDON ROCKET

Sisymbrium irio

Hedge Mustard

Features: London rocket is a mild member of the mustard family. One of the first greens available in spring, the young plants consist of low-growing rosettes of deeply pinnate leaves with large terminal lobes. Flower stalks grow 1 to 2 feet tall and are crowned with small clusters of tiny, yellow, 4-petaled flowers, which are followed by long, narrow, upright seedpods growing along the flower stalks. London rocket grows in disturbed places in Europe, North Africa, the Near East, and throughout the United States. The best time to gather the leaves is spring.

Facts: Mustard is a member of the cruciferous family of plants which are believed to contain anti-cancer properties. Table mustard is made from mustard seeds which are ground up and mixed with vinegar, cream and spices. Not all mustard seeds are good for making mustard.

Foods:
Raw: Mustard leaves, flowers, stems and seeds can be eaten raw, but because they're hot and spicy, they make a better seasoning than food.

Cooked: All parts of London rocket can be eaten cooked. The cooked leaves are milder than the raw ones. Mustard seeds and flowers remain spicy even after cooking. Milk helps to neutralize the bitter flavor.

CREAM OF MUSTARD SOUP
(Serves 2 – 4)

1/2 cup water
4 - 8 cups London rocket greens, chopped
2 tablespoons butter
2 cloves garlic, minced
1 onion, diced
2 tablespoons flour
2 cups broth or water
1 cup milk
Juice of 1/2 lemon
Salt and pepper

Boil 1/2 cup water. Add greens, cover and steam for 5 minutes. Lower the heat if necessary to prevent burning. Drain greens and set them aside. Melt butter in a large pot and sauté garlic and onion until clear. Slowly stir in flour and gradually add broth or water, stir well. Bring to a gentle boil and stir in greens. Cover. Turn down heat and simmer for 5 minutes. Add milk and heat; but do not boil. Stir in lemon juice and season with salt and pepper.

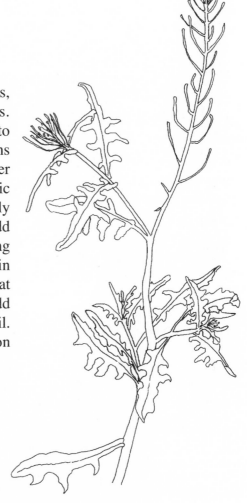

MANZANITA

Arctostaphylos glauca

Features: There are roughly 38 different species of manzanita, ranging in size from low shrubs to small trees. They're characterized by twisted branches and rich red bark that is sometimes shredded. *Arctostaphylos glauca* is an evergreen shrub with long, somewhat narrow leaves with smooth margins. Some of the other species have leaves that are more ovate. All manzanita leaves are stiff, and most point conspicuously upward. Tiny, urn-shaped, white or pink flowers hang in small clusters from the ends of branches. Manzanita berries come in a variety of colors and sizes ranging from pea-sized and red, to larger, oval, brownish-red ones. They also vary in palatability. I've found that the smaller red fruit are usually sweetest. Most manzanita berries resemble dry apples in texture.

Facts: Manzanitas grow throughout the West in chaparral and dry environments but not in deserts. Their berries ripen in spring. The name "manzanita" comes from the Spanish word *manzana*, which means "apple." *Ita* is a diminutive which means "small." Hence "manzanita" means "little apple" —an apt description of the fruit. Although people sometimes call manzanita, "bearberry," this name usually refers to *Arctostaphylos alpina*, a small shrub which grows in arctic and alpine regions. The Miwok Indians of Yosemite Valley left the berries on the bushes until they were dry. Then they gathered and ground the berries, seeds and all, and poured water over them; later collecting the resulting liquid, which they drank.

Foods:
Tea: Crumble 2 to 3 leaves and place them into a cup. Fill with boiling water. Cover and steep for 5 minutes. Strain, sweeten and serve. This tea is said to have slightly disinfectant properties.

Raw: All manzanita berries can be eaten raw, but some taste better than others.

Dried: They can be dried and stored for future use.

MANZANITA BERRY CIDER
(Makes 1 quart)

      4 cups manzanita berries, washed
      Water
      Sugar or honey

Place berries in a saucepan and cover with water. Boil until soft. Drain and bruise them, but don't crush them. Measure the berries and place them into a bowl with an equal amount of water. Cover and let sit all day. Then strain out the berries but retain the liquid. Refrigerate the liquid until sediment settles at the bottom. Strain out the sediment and sweeten the remaining juice with sugar or honey. Dilute if desired.

MESQUITE

Prosopis glandulosa

Honey Mesquite

Features: Mesquites are large deciduous shrubs or small trees with numerous brittle branches. They grow 9 to 20 feet high and have hanging, fern-like leaves and sweetly scented, yellow-green flowers which crowd together in cylindrical patterns along flower spikes. Honey mesquites also have pairs of long, sharp, straight spines along their branches. Seedpods, hanging in small clusters, resemble long, lumpy, green beans. The young pods are initially green, becoming yellow and brown with age.

Facts: Mesquites grow along washes, usually at elevations below 4,000 feet, except in the Colorado and Mojave deserts, where they have been found growing at higher elevations. Mature seedpods are available during late summer and early fall. Southwestern Native Americans relied heavily upon mesquites for food and other uses. The pods and seeds, which are high in sugar and extremely nutritious, were prepared in several different ways. Because they contain 1/3 sugar they are very sweet, and were a welcome addition to a basically bland diet. Native Americans used gum from the bark as candy or hair dye. Sometimes they even mixed the sap with mud in order to kill lice.

Foods:
Tea: Put 8 or 9 green or dry yellow twigs into a cup. Fill with boiling water. Cover and steep 20 minutes. Strain and serve for a sweet mild tea. Another method is to boil 8 pods in 2 cups of water for 1 hour. Mash the pods, strain and serve. Both teas have a delicate vanilla scent and flavor requiring no sweetening. These teas are sometimes used to treat diarrhea, dysentery, and stomach ulcers.

Raw: Gum from the bark and the soft interior of the pods can be eaten raw. A cold beverage is made by soaking seeds or pods in water for several hours.

Cooked: The pods, with or without the seeds, can be ground into meal. This is not easy because the pods are soft and the seeds are hard. Native Americans used a special wooden mortar made out of cottonwood to grind them. First dry the pods in an oven or the sun and then grind them in a blender or food processor. It's easier if you grind the pods without the seeds, but you lose a lot of nutrition that way. Traditionally, the resulting meal was used to make mush or mixed with water and slowly heated in an oven or sunshine to make cakes. The cakes were stored and later used as needed to make mush or beverages. Currently, some people like to use the pods to flavor their grills for barbecues, a practice that is much less destructive than using mesquite briquettes.

CAHUILLA MESQUITE DESERT BREAD
(Serves 6 - 8)

> Mesquite flour
> Water

Mix a few drops of water with a small amount of flour. Add more flour, then more water, little by little. Shape into a small loaf. Bake in the sun.

(Recipe reprinted with permission from Malki Museum's *Native Foods Tasting Experience*. Edited by Alice Kotzen (Banning, AL Malki Museum Press, 1994).

MILKWEED

Asclepias spp.

Silkweed

Features: There are over 100 species of milkweed in the world, and at least 25 of them are native to the United States. Most milkweeds are toxic to some degree, especially the narrow-leaved varieties. Only 3 of the wide-leaved varieties were generally used for food, and they require careful preparation. These broad-leaved varieties are annuals and have soft, fuzzy, faded grayish-green leaves and stems. Large felt-like leaves grow opposite each other along thick upright or somewhat prostrate stems. There are terminal clusters of small, attractive, white or purplish, 5-petaled, bell-shaped flowers. Distinctive milkweed pods are large and fuzzy, containing numerous downy, dandelion-like seeds. Although the flowers of narrow-leaved milkweed *(Asclepias fascicularis)* were eaten raw, in moderation, by some Native Americans, this species is considered toxic. It is not difficult to distinguish between the edible broad-leaved milkweed and the toxic narrow-leaved varieties. Broad-leaved milkweed has fuzzy broad leaves, larger, more rounded, fuzz-covered seedpods, and pale purple or white flowers, as well as a stouter, fuzzy stem.

Facts: During late summer, mature milkweeds can be found growing by roadsides or in open spaces, such as meadows, throughout the United States. Native Americans used milkweed for many purposes in addition to food. String and fishnets were made from the fibers of its stems, and the sap of edible species was made into chewing gum or applied to warts. Milkweed seeds were ground and used medicinally for rattlesnake bites or for saddle sores on horses.

Foods:
USE WITH CAUTION.

Remember, these recipes are only for the edible varieties.

Raw: In summer the flowers of edible varieties are sometimes gathered and eaten raw or cooked.

Cooked: Young shoots less than 6 inches tall, which are often available during late spring, can be steamed or boiled. Newly opened leaves can be cooked like spinach. Cooked, unopened flower buds taste similar to broccoli. Small tender pods, which are still firm to the touch, can also be cooked and eaten. They begin to mature during summer. All parts require cooking in more than 1 change of water in order to remove their bitterness. The trick is to know how many changes are needed and not to overcook the milkweed. First boil water, and then add whichever part you're cooking. Cover and boil for only 1 minute. Drain. Add new boiling water to the pot. (It saves time if you already have water boiling in a second pot or teakettle). Boil again for only 1 minute. Drain. Repeat this procedure at least one more time. The final time, boil for 10 minutes, then drain and season with butter and salt.

BOILED MILKWEED SEEDPODS
(Serves 2)

8 firm seedpods (1 to 2 inches long)
Water
Salt and pepper
Butter

Clean the seedpods. Heat water to boiling and add the milkweed pods. Cover and cook until tender. Season to taste with salt and pepper. Serve with butter. Milkweed seedpods are really good! It's a challenge to find enough pods before they get too mature.

MINER'S LETTUCE

Claytonia perfoliata

Features: Miner's Lettuce is a truly unique plant. Appearing soon after winter rains, the young plants consist of a cluster of small, upright, spatulate-shaped leaves, each on its own stem. The somewhat shiny green leaves that follow are disc-like, and each is pierced by a flower stalk. Small clusters of tiny, white, 5-petaled flowers grow at the top of these stalks. The blossoms slowly open as the stalks continue to grow. Mature miner's lettuce clusters grow from 3 to 12 inches tall. Young plants are tastiest. Miner's lettuce is available from early spring until midsummer if there is sufficient water.

Facts: *Claytonia perfoliata* is common in moist, shady places throughout North America. Miner's lettuce got its name from the gold miners of the 1840s. They didn't have time to garden, and miner's lettuce was one of the few edible greens which they utilized. It's said that they preferred it wilted—smothered with hot

bacon grease. Because miner's lettuce is high in vitamin C, it was a sometimes eaten as a scurvy preventative.

Foods:

Tea: Crush a few leaves and place them into a cup. Fill the cup with boiling water. Cover and steep for 5 minutes. Strain, sweeten and serve. (This tea should be drunk in moderation—Native Americans used it as a laxative).

Raw: Miner's lettuce is delicious raw, especially before the flowers appear. It makes a great snack and a tasty addition to salads.

Cooked: Miner's lettuce is good stir-fried or steamed, but greatly decreases in volume when cooked.

MINER'S LETTUCE SALAD
(Serves 2)

> 2 cups miner's lettuce leaves, cleaned and torn
> 1 tomato, diced
> 1/4 onion, chopped
> 1/2 cup feta
> 1/4 cup vinaigrette dressing

Mix all ingredients together and enjoy.

VINAIGRETTE DRESSING
(Makes 1 cup)

> 1/2 cup oil (olive or canola)
> 1/4 cup apple cider vinegar
> 1/2 cup water
> 3 cloves garlic, crushed
> Pinch of paprika
> 1/2 teaspoon basil
> Salt and pepper

Blend all ingredients together. Season to taste with salt and pepper.

MINT

Mentha spp.

Mountain Mint

Features: Mints are perennial, aromatic herbs with square stems which grow up to 3 feet high. Mint leaves grow opposite each other along the stems. The variety pictured, which is sometimes called "mountain mint", has slightly hairy, dark green, toothed leaves. When it matures, small branches appear opposite each other at the junction of some of the leaves and stems. Then small clusters of lavender flowers appear at the ends of the branches. Not all mints are branched. Flowers from unbranched mints grow in whorls around the top section of the stems.

Facts: Since mints require a moist environment, they are often found growing in or near streams throughout the United States. Young plants and new leaves appear during spring, but the flowers don't usually bloom until midsummer. Mint tea is known to be soothing for upset stomachs and is sometimes used to quiet fussy babies. Mint is also a breath freshener and very high in vitamins A, C, and K, as well as calcium and manganese. If only the top of a plant is harvested, it will continue to produce new growth.

Foods:
Tea: Put several fresh leaves or 1 teaspoon dried leaves into a cup. Add boiling water. Cover and steep for 5 minutes. Strain and sweeten if desired.

Raw: Mint leaves are refreshing right off the plant. They taste good in salads, drinks, and desserts. A few leaves can be added to a canteen to flavor the water.

Cooked: Mint leaves are often cooked with meats and vegetables, especially in the Near East.

TABBOULEH
(Serves 4 – 6)

3/4 cup bulgur wheat
1 cup water
3 tablespoons extra virgin olive oil
2 to 3 lemons, juiced
1 bunch parsley, chopped
2 tablespoons fresh mint, chopped
2 tomatoes, chopped
1 bunch scallions, minced
1/2 onion, grated or chopped
1 green pepper, minced (optional)
1 head romaine lettuce

Rinse bulgur wheat and soak it for 30 minutes in water. Drain it and stir in the oil and lemon juice. Then add all the remaining ingredients except lettuce. Put the tabbouleh into a mound on the center of a plate. Arrange the lettuce around it. Use the lettuce to scoop up the tabbouleh and eat them together.

YOGURT SALAD WITH MINT
(Serves 2 – 4)

2 cups yogurt
1 cucumber, grated
1 tbs. lemon juice
2 cloves garlic, minced
2 tbs. fresh mint leaves, chopped
1/2 tsp. fresh dill, chopped
Salt (optional)

Combine all ingredients except salt. Add salt only if desired. Chill and serve. This yogurt goes well with falafels.

MONKEY FLOWER

Mimulus guttatus

Common Monkey Flower, Large Monkey Flower,
Yellow Monkey Flower

Features: Monkey Flowers are annual spring plants. There are over 150 species of monkey flowers worldwide; about 27 of them are in California. *Mimulus guttatus,* also known as "yellow monkey flower", has the largest flowers and the largest, tastiest leaves of this family. These somewhat rounded leaves have toothed margins and grow opposite each other. Each leaf or leaf cluster grows on its own leaf stem. The irregular yellow flowers are 2-lipped, with the lower lip larger than the upper, and have hairy throats with red spots above. When they first appear, young *M. guttatus* plants consist of a bunch of upright leaves growing directly from the ground. The height of monkey flower plants varies greatly depending on how well they are shaded and watered. Most of the plants I have encountered were 6 to 18 inches tall by the time they blossomed. Many people believe that the flowers resemble monkey faces.

Facts: Common monkey flower grows in shallow streams and moist places throughout the West, especially after a good rainy season. The best time to gather it is in spring. Early settlers and Native Americans both used yellow monkey flower plants for food. The stems and leaves were eaten raw or cooked. Crushed leaves were used for poultices, and roots were utilized as an astringent. Other varieties of monkey flower, which grow in drier environments, have small flowers, sticky stems, and small sticky leaves. These varieties don't taste good.

Foods:
Raw: Young stems and leaves can be eaten fresh in salads and sandwiches. These tender leaves taste like lettuce; however, after the plants flower, they become less palatable. Monkey flower blossoms are a colorful addition to salads and Jell-O molds.

Cooked: Young monkey flower stems and leaves can be steamed, boiled, stir-fried, or added to soups.

MONKEY FLOWER SALAD
(Serves 4)

> 1 head lettuce, chopped
> 1 cup monkey flower leaves, chopped
> 3 scallions, minced
> 1 red pepper, diced
> Vinaigrette dressing (see page 77)
> Several monkey flower blossoms

Mix all ingredients together, except flowers. Garnish the finished salad with flowers.

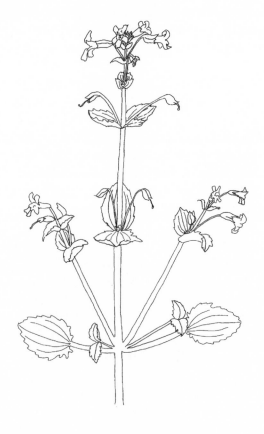

MULLEIN

Verbascum thapsus

Wooly Mullein, Velvet Dock

Features: Mullein is generally a biennial that usually grows 3 or 4 feet high but can reach up to 8 feet in height, towering above other plants in fields and byways. Its stout stalk, adorned with numerous small bright yellow flowers, is very conspicuous. During its first year, mullein has no flower stalk, only a ground-level rosette of large, soft, pale grayish-green leaves which grow up to 2 feet long. During the second year, its upright flower stalk appears. Although usually unbranched, this stalk may have as many as 5 upright branches, resembling a candelabra. The leaves diminish in size as they grow toward the top of the stalk; they also become more vertical and less horizontal than those farther down. Tight, yellow flower buds bunch together along the top of the sometimes forked flower stalk.

Facts: Mullein grows in waste places throughout the West and blooms during summer. All parts are mildly toxic except for the flowers. However, this plant was used medicinally, especially for respiratory ailments. Mohican Indians used to smoke the leaves to relieve asthma and coughs. Navajos blended them with regular tobacco to treat mild mental disorders. Mullein leaves were also softened on hot rocks and used to relieve foot pain. Tea made from the roots is said to help with liver trouble.

Foods:
Tea: Put a few inches of crushed leaf into a cup. Fill with boiling water. Cover and steep for 10 minutes. Strain, sweeten, and serve. This tea is said to give relief for bronchial infections. For a sweeter tea, use the flowers. Steep 5-10 flowers in hot water until the water turns yellow. Strain out the flowers and drink the remaining liquid either hot or cold for coughs, congestion, and hoarseness.

MUSTARD

Brassica nigra

Black Mustard

Features: Black mustard, an annual, is very common in open fields and chaparral. In spring, masses of its yellow flowers cover the hills. Young plants consist of a rosette of coarse deeply-lobed leaves with large terminal lobes, growing close to the ground. A stiff, slender, much-branched flower stalk rises 3 to 6 feet high from the center of the rosette. Clusters of tiny, yellow, 4-petaled flowers grow at the tips of the branches.

Facts: Black mustard was originally brought to California by mission fathers who planted this hardy, conspicuous plant between the different missions so that travelers wouldn't get lost. The dried mustard powder sold in stores for external use as a mustard plaster is prepared from black mustard seeds. A mustard plaster is made by mixing mustard powder with flour and water. Then it's heated and applied to the chest to relieve congestion. Mustard leaves contain vitamins: A, B1 and B2.

Foods:
Raw: Young stems, leaves, and flowers can be eaten raw as a trail snack or mixed in a salad.

Cooked: Black mustard leaves can be cooked in most recipes calling for strong-flavored greens. Young, lower leaves are the mildest and most tender, requiring about 30 minutes of steaming or boiling before they are ready to eat. The unopened flower buds can be steamed for 15–20 minutes and used as a spice.

GRANDMA'S GREEN SOUP
(Serves 2 – 4)

1 1/2 tablespoons extra virgin olive oil
1/2 onion, sliced
1 clove garlic, minced
2 cups water or broth
1 potato, cubed
1 cup young mustard leaves, chopped
3 cups lamb's quarters or amaranth greens, chopped
1 teaspoon thyme
1 teaspoon basil
Salt and pepper
1 cup milk
1 tablespoon butter
1/4 cup Parmesan

Heat olive oil and sauté onion and garlic until clear. Add water or broth and bring to a boil. Stir in potato. Cover, lower heat, and cook for 10 minutes. Add mustard leaves, cover, and cook for 10 more minutes. Add the mild greens and seasonings. Cover and cook for 5 minutes. Then add milk and simmer. Stir in the butter and cheese.

NASTURTIUM

Tropaeolum majus

Features: Nasturtiums are perennial trailing vines or delicate climbing clusters of brilliantly-hued red, yellow, orange, burgundy or variegated flowers. It's next to impossible to find a solitary plant. Often they can be found carpeting large sunny areas where the soil is poor and dry. Nasturtiums have distinctive leaves which are in the shape of irregular rounds. Delicate white veins are arranged like the spokes of a wheel and meet at a central point on the leaves. A weak stem grows directly beneath this point. Colorful flowers with 5 large, overlapping petals grow singly, each on a fragile stem.

Facts: Nasturtiums grow throughout the United States. The leaves and flowers taste best when gathered from young plants—usually during spring and summer. These plants are surprisingly nutritious. The leaves contain iron, sulfur, and vitamin C. Sailors, who needed a lot of vitamin C in order to prevent scurvy, sometimes used nasturtium leaves as a remedy. Insects don't like this plant, and it's often used as a companion plant to keep insects away from its tastier neighbors.

Foods:
Raw: All parts can be eaten raw. The leaves and flowers are both spicy and add a lot of flavor to sandwiches. They taste really good combined with bread and butter or cream cheese sandwiches. Nasturtium flowers make a colorful addition to salads and Jell-O molds. The seedpods, known as "poor man's capers," can be used raw or in recipes calling for capers.

NASTURTIUM SALAD

(Serves 2)

> 1/2 cucumber, cubed
> 1 tomato, diced
> 6 - 8 young nasturtium leaves, chopped
> Vinaigrette dressing (see page 77)
> 2 - 4 nasturtium flowers

Mix vegetables. Add dressing to taste, arrange on plates, and garnish with nasturtium blossoms.

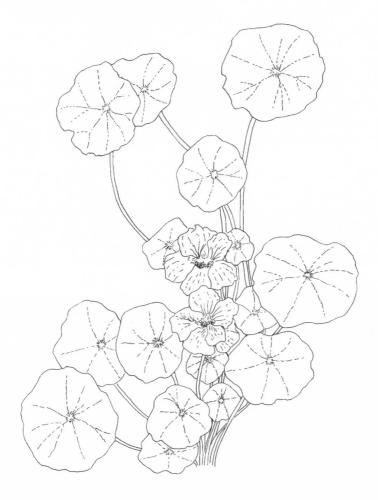

OAKS

Quercus spp.

Features: There are over 300 different species of oak trees in the world! Since they cross-pollinate, it's not always simple to identify a specific species. Fortunately, the acorns of all oak trees are edible if properly prepared. Different varieties of oaks have crops every 1, 2, or 3 years, or irregularly. These crops vary in quantity and quality. Oaks can be either deciduous or evergreen, ranging in size from small shrubs to large trees. Their small, yellowish-white flowers hang in drooping clusters, developing into acorns by the end of summer.

Facts: Acorns are very nutritious, containing: protein, fat, calcium, magnesium, phosphorus, potassium, and sulfur. They were an important food source for Native Americans. Acorns from the black oak were the favorite of the Miwoks of Yosemite Valley. After the acorns were gathered, they were often stored for future use. Before they could be eaten, all the tannic acid had to be leached out. It was a time-consuming process. Today, a simpler method is to shell the acorns, chop them, put them in water and boil. Change the water every 10 or 15 minutes and continue boiling until the water is relatively clear and the acorns no longer taste bitter. Keep 2 pots of water boiling, and after you drain the one containing acorns you will be able to refill it with already hot water from the other.

Foods:
Cooked: Acorn meal can be leached, finely ground, and used to make hot mush. Boil 2 cups of water and stir in 1 cup of the acorn meal. Cover and cook over low heat until it is the desired consistency. Don't forget to stir. Cover, cool, and serve. Chopped, leached acorns can be used in recipes calling for nuts.

ACORNY CHOCOLATE CHIP COOKIES
(Makes 2 - 3 dozen)

> 2 cups flour
> 1 teaspoon baking soda
> 1 teaspoon salt
> 1 1/2 sticks butter, melted
> 1 1/2 cups sugar
> 1 teaspoon vanilla
> 3 eggs, beaten
> 6 ounces chocolate chips
> 1 cup acorns, chopped and leached.

Mix flour, baking soda, and salt together. Add the butter, sugar, vanilla, and eggs. Stir until well blended. Add chips and acorns. Drop by spoonful onto a well-greased cookie sheet. Bake at 375° for 15 minutes or until done.

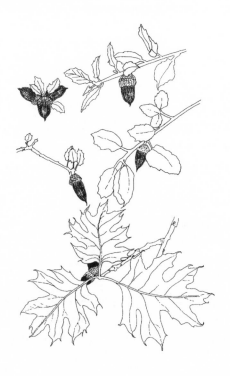

ORACH

Atriplex patula

Features: Annual orach is one of my favorite wild plants. It often appears almost vine-like with its slender, fragile, 1 to 2 1/2 foot long stalks. Sometimes it grows upright, while at other times it almost sprawls along the ground. Its dark green leaves are halbert-shaped and grow opposite each other along stems and branches. Pairs of smaller leaves spring up on short stems at the juncture of the larger leaves and the stalk. The green flowers are small and inconspicuous. Orach leaves resemble spinach both in appearance and flavor.

Facts: Orach grows near water in coastal salt marshes or in other moist locations throughout the Pacific Northwest. This prolific plant is first available in late spring and can be collected throughout summer. It's high in iron and extremely nutritious. Because orach is a member of the saltbush family, it's also slightly salty, and was a welcome addition to the diets of many Native Americans.

Foods:
Raw: The leaves are delicious eaten raw as a snack or in sandwiches and salads. But when it grows near water of unknown purity, it needs to be washed well before it is eaten.

Cooked: The entire plant can be steamed, boiled, stir-fried, or added to omelets. It cooks quickly and should not be overcooked because it shrinks. Since orach is salty, taste your dish first before adding salt.

ORACH QUICHE Á LA GRECQUE
(Serves 4 - 6)

Crust:
1 cup flour
4 tablespoons butter
2 - 4 tablespoons ice water

Prepare crust. Put it in a greased pie pan and bake at 375° for 10 minutes, then set it aside.

3/4 cup feta, crumbled
1/2 cup cottage cheese
1/2 onion, chopped
1 tablespoon extra virgin olive oil
1 teaspoon dry basil
1 dash freshly grated nutmeg
1 clove garlic, minced
1/2 cup milk
4 eggs
1 1/2 cups orach greens, chopped

Blend all ingredients together except milk, eggs, and greens. Stir in the milk and eggs, than add the greens. Pour into crust and bake at 400° for 20 minutes. Lower heat to 350° and bake for 15 to 20 minutes more or until done. Cool for 10 minutes before serving.

PINEAPPLE WEED

Matricaria matricariodes

Features: Pineapple weed is a tiny, low-growing, annual herb which can grow 3 to 8 inches high, but usually is much shorter. It has a stiff, slightly-branched stem and delicate fern-like, much-divided leaves. Flower heads grow at the end of the stems and branches. They resemble small, yellow, oval balls, and are made up entirely of disc flowers with no ray flowers (petals). Pineapple weed sometimes appears as early as February in southern California, but not until March or later in other southwestern states. It is often mistaken for chamomile, *(M. chamomilla)* because they are similar in flavor and use. However, their appearances are not the same. Chamomile is much taller than pineapple weed and its flowers have petals. Chamomile is not native to the Southwest, but pineapple weed is.

Facts: Pineapple weed is common in barren waste places in the Southwest. When crushed, it emits a mild odor that some people say smells like pineapples.

Foods:
Tea: The whole plant can be used for tea, but it is sweeter if only the flowers are used. Like chamomile tea, pineapple weed tea is mild and said to be soothing for upset stomachs and nerves, and helpful in treating colds. Put 2 tablespoons of flowers into a cup. Fill with boiling water. Cover and steep for 10 minutes. Strain, sweeten, and serve.

Raw: Pineapple weed can be eaten as a snack or added to salads. It has a very mild flavor. Be sure to rinse off all the dust before you eat it.

Cooked: The entire plant can be steamed, boiled, or added to soups and stews.

Dried: Pineapple weed is easy to dry and can be stored for future use. It's best to store it in a dark place in order to preserve its flavor and medicinal properties.

PLANTAIN

Plantago major

Common Plantain, Broad-Leafed Plantain

Features: There are many species of perennial plantain. Broad-leafed *(P. major)* and narrow-leafed plantain *(P. lanceolata)* are the most common varieties. *P. major* grows largest where there's an ample supply of water. Young plants consist of a rosette of large ovate leaves which terminate in a point. Typical of all plantain leaves, the veins are parallel. Small clusters of inconspicuous flowers cover the upper part of impressive flower stalks which may grow as high as 18 inches. The small brown seeds which follow are densely packed.

Facts: Plantain can be found growing in moist locations throughout the Unites States. Spring is the best time to gather the leaves. Broad-leaved plantain is an introduced plant, not a native. Its leaves are rich in vitamin C and other minerals. Native Americans used to call this plant "The White Man's Footsteps" because it appeared wherever the settlers went.

Foods:
Tea: Save and drink the liquid from cooked greens or add 1 cup of boiling water to 1/3 cup of crushed leaves. Cover and steep for 5 minutes. Strain, sweeten, and serve.

Raw: In spring, young leaves can be eaten raw or added to salads and sandwiches. Although older leaves are edible, they become stringy and often bitter. New leaves are always best and have a pleasant lettuce-like flavor. Plantain seeds, which are related to psyllium, can be used as a laxative. Just soak them in water until it becomes cloudy, and then drink the liquid, seeds and all.

Cooked: Plantain leaves can be steamed, boiled, sautéed, or added to soups and stews. If the leaves are bitter, their flavor can be improved by boiling in 2 changes of water. Honey can be added.

Tender leaves only need to be steamed for 3 minutes before they're ready.

GREEK SALAD
(Serves 4)

1 cup young plantain leaves, chopped
1 1/2 tomatoes, chopped
1/2 cucumber, diced
1/2 onion, minced
1/2 cup green pepper, diced (optional)
8 ounces feta, cubed
Olives (optional)
1/4 cup vinaigrette dressing (see page 77)

Clean the plantain well if it was gathered near a questionable water source. Combine all the ingredients and serve with pita bread.

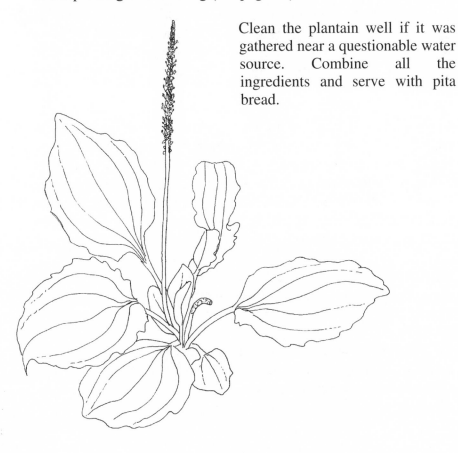

PRICKLY LETTUCE

Lactuca scariola

Compass Plant

Features: You can't miss annual prickly lettuce. Although it usually grows only a foot high, *Lactuca scariola* can grow up to 8 feet tall! Initially, prickly lettuce is topped by a bunch of leaves which spread out in all directions — much resembling a "bad hair day." These large, dark green leaves become less conspicuous as the plant matures. At first, new leaves hug the unbranched stalk, later they begin jutting out in the four directions of the compass. These slightly lobed, irregularly toothed leaves are easily distinguished by a row of small prickles along their spine. Tiny clusters of small, yellow, dandelion-like flowers on short upright stems grow at the top of the stalk. When they go to seed they become white and fluffy, again resembling small dandelion blooms.

Facts: Prickly lettuce grows best in fields, clearings, and other slightly moist environments throughout the United States. New plants are available in spring and occasionally early summer. Different varieties of lettuce have been cultivated for ages. Ancient Egyptians, Greeks and Romans all cultivated and ate various types of lettuce. Lettuce is reputed to have a tranquilizing effect when eaten in quantity, especially the sap.

Foods:
Raw: Young leaves can be eaten raw, but they tend to be quite bitter unless they are very small.

Cooked: Young leaves, flowers, and tender stems can be boiled, steamed, or sautéed. If they are old or bitter, they taste better if they are boiled in 2 changes of water.

PRICKLY LETTUCE IN CREAM SAUCE
(Serves 2)

>   2 cups water
>   2 cups prickly lettuce leaves, cleaned and chopped
>   1 cup water

Boil 2 cups of water. Add prickly lettuce. Cover and cook for 10 minutes. Drain and set aside. Boil 1 cup of fresh water. Add the cooked greens. Cover and cook for 5 minutes more. Drain and serve with white sauce.

WHITE SAUCE
(Serves 2)

>   1 tablespoon butter
>   2 tablespoons flour
>   1 cup milk
>   Salt and pepper

Melt butter and gradually stir in flour. Slowly add milk, stirring constantly. Season to taste with salt and pepper.

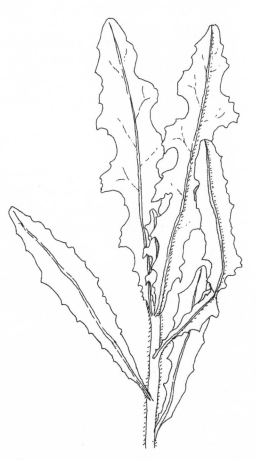

PRICKLY PEAR

Opuntia littoralis

Features: There are about 250 different varieties of perennial prickly pear cactus! Fortunately, all of them are edible. They're characterized by large, flat, jointed pads which are dotted with glochids, (small, irritating barbed spines which grow in shallow indentations known as areoles). Some varieties also have larger spines as well. Large, lovely flowers, (which are usually yellow, but sometimes apricot or even red), grow side-by-side along the top edge of the terminal joints, maturing into green, light bulb-shaped fruits which become red or reddish-purple when ripe. These "pears" are also adorned with minute glochids. Prickly pears can reach the size of a small tree, but usually are much smaller.

Facts: Prickly pears grow in desert and chaparral environments throughout the world. The fruit of most varieties ripens at the end of summer when they become sweet and juicy. Although both fruit and young pads are edible, care should be taken in gathering them. There are many gathering techniques, but one of the simplest is to use a bag and a barbecue fork. Hold a heavy paper bag underneath the part being harvested, and use the fork to break it off. If the little hairs get into your hands they can be quite irritating. The spines and glochids on the pads can be scraped off with a knife, singed off in a fire, or the pears can be plunged into boiling water for 1 minute, transferred to cold water, and peeled by hand. The softened hairs do not present a problem, but dry loose hairs on the working surface do. So, be very careful if you choose this method.

Foods:
Raw: The ripe fruits, known as "pears" or "tunas," can be eaten raw after all the hairs have been removed. Most varieties are sweet and juicy.

Cooked: They can also be cooked to make jams, jellies, or syrups. The pads, known as *nopalitos* or *nopales*, can be cooked after the spines and hairs are removed. They're good mixed in salsa, rice, beans or added to scrambled eggs, although their texture is somewhat mucilaginous.

TUNA JUICE
(Makes 1 quart)

> 24 tunas
> 1 cup sugar
> 1 quart water

Peel the tunas, (using boiling water), and crush in a container. Strain the juice and then mix the juice, sugar and water together. Chill and serve. Tuna juice is rich and sweet—almost a syrup. It combines well with other fruit juices or carbonated beverages.

NOPALES
(Serves 4)

> 4 young cactus pads
> 2 cups water

Over a newspaper, scrape the spines carefully from the pads with a knife. Wipe the knife constantly. Rinse and cube the pads, then add to a pot of boiling water. Boil until tender, about 15 minutes. Serve with salsa and corn tortillas.

PRICKLY SOW THISTLE

Sonchus asper

Wild Lettuce

Features: Annual prickly sow thistle is an erect, branched plant that grows 1 to 5 feet tall. Prickly leaves grow along the young stem, hugging it at the leaves' bases and then extending outward. As the plant grows and matures, the new leaves decrease in size and grow farther apart from each other as they approach the terminal ends of stem and branches. The tips of the mature stem and branches are bare of leaves, but support several small yellow, dandelion-like flowers.

Facts: Prickly sow thistle grows in open spaces throughout the west. It's available from late winter until fall. Because the sap from several varieties of wild lettuce is thought to be sedative in nature, it's been used in the past to help treat opium addiction.

Foods:
Raw: Young leaves (before flowers appear), and young flower stalks (peeled), can be eaten raw. Their flavor is surprisingly mild, much milder than prickly lettuce.

Cooked: Young leaves and young peeled flower stalks can be steamed or boiled until tender. The leaves cook in about 3 minutes but the stalks require 5–10 minutes. Both are tasty served with orange or lemon flavored melted butter.

PRICKLY SOW THISTLE STIR-FRY
(Serves 2 – 4)

   2 tablespoons oil
   2 cloves garlic, minced
   1 onion, sliced
   2 stalks celery, sliced
   2 carrots, sliced diagonally
   1- 2 cups young prickly sow thistle leaves, cleaned
   Soy sauce
   Salt and pepper

Heat oil and sauté garlic and onion until clear. Stir in celery and carrots. Heat over medium heat for 3-4 minutes. Stir in prickly sow thistle leaves and sprinkle with soy sauce. Add water, if necessary, to prevent burning. Cover and cook for 4 minutes. Season with salt and pepper and serve over rice.

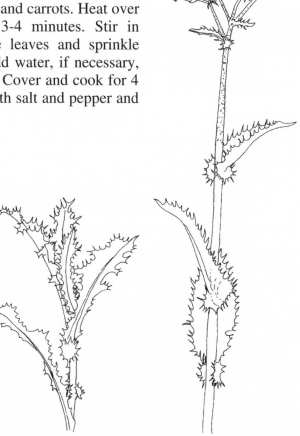

PROSTRATE PIGWEED

Amaranthus californicus

Features: Annual prostrate pigweed is actually a prostrate amaranth. It sprawls over the ground forming colorful mats of small green spatulate-shaped leaves and succulent reddish-purple stems. This tasty plant spreads outward rather than upward and rarely grows over a few inches high. Leaves with wavy margins grow in clusters alternately along stems and branches.

Facts: *Amaranthus californicus* grows in waste places, fields, and cultivated soil throughout the United States. Although available from spring through summer, it always tastes best when picked young. All members of the amaranth family are edible and extremely nutritious. Whole plants were an important part of the diet of southwestern Native Americans. Amaranths also produce copious quantities of small seeds which can be harvested and used for flour or mush.

Foods:
Raw: Young leaves can be eaten raw or added to sandwiches and salads.

Cooked: Prostrate pigweed can be steamed, boiled, sautéed, or stir-fried. The flavor is pleasantly mild, and mixes well with other greens.

AFRICAN PEANUT SOUP
(Serves 4 – 6)

> 2 tablespoons butter
> 1 onion, minced
> 2 tablespoons flour
> 4 cups chicken broth or water
> 1/4 cup peanut butter (ground peanuts and salt)
> 2 cups prostrate pigweed greens, cleaned

1/2 teaspoon chili powder
2 teaspoons curry powder
1 teaspoon salt
Dash of red pepper

Melt butter and sauté onion until clear. Slowly stir in flour. Add broth or water gradually and mix well. Stir in peanut butter. Add greens. Season with chili powder, curry powder, salt and pepper. Cover and simmer for 5 more minutes. Traditionally, this is served over rice; more as a sauce than a soup. Condiments such as peanuts, shredded coconut, bananas, and chopped green onions can be served in separate dishes.

PIGWEED OMELET
(Serves 2)

1 tablespoon butter
1 garlic clove, minced
1/2 onion, chopped
1 cup prostrate pigweed greens, chopped
2 eggs, beaten
Salt and pepper

Melt butter in a frying pan. Sauté garlic and onion until clear. Stir in greens. Add eggs and brown lightly. Flip and heat until firm. Season with salt and pepper and serve immediately.

PURSLANE

Portulaca oleracea

Pusley

Features: Purslane is a creeping, low-growing annual succulent that spreads out from a central taproot and forms mats 1 to 2 inches high along the ground. Flat, somewhat paddle-shaped leaves grow both singly and in clusters along stems and branches. Tiny, bright yellow flowers grow at the juncture of stems and leaves, blooming for only a few hours each day when there is sufficient sunshine.

Facts: Purslane is generally available from spring through autumn. All parts are edible. It grows throughout the United States in sandy soil, cultivated lawns, and waste places. If only the tips are gathered, the plants will continue to produce new growth. Pueblo Indians used to gather tiny prolific purslane seeds, possibly to combine them with other seeds and cook as mush, or to grind into flour for bread. Purslane is very nutritious. Not only does it contain a high percentage of protein, carbohydrates, and omega-3 fatty acids, but it's also high in calcium and vitamin C when raw, and riboflavin and B-6 when cooked.

Foods:
Raw: Purslane can be munched along the trail or added to salads and dips. Young growth is tastiest, with a refreshing, slightly tart flavor.

Cooked: The entire plant can be steamed, boiled, or added to soups and stews. Because it tends to be mucilaginous, purslane is sometimes used as a thickener.

Dried: Portulaca oleracea can also be slowly dried in the sun or an oven, and saved for future use.

MEXICAN STYLE PURSLANE SALAD
(Serves 2 – 4)

> 1 cup young stems and leaves, cleaned and chopped
> 1/2 onion, sliced
> 1 cup tomatoes, diced
> 1/2 cup cilantro, chopped
> Vinaigrette dressing or salsa

Mix, chill, and serve. This is an excellent side dish for spicy Mexican food.

SERVICEBERRY

Amelanchier spp.

Juneberry, Shadblow, Sarviceberry

Features: There are about 15 different species of serviceberries, ranging in size from bushy shrubs 5 feet high to trees up to 20 feet tall. They're usually found growing in thickets. All serviceberry plants produce edible berries that become dark blue or purplish-black when ripe and are filled with many seeds. Large white flowers gather in small clusters, accompanied by green leaves which grow alternately along the branches. Each leaf is almost entirely round except for its tip which is flat and serrated, resembling a crewcut. The leaves turn yellow each autumn.

Facts: Serviceberries begin ripening as early as late spring and continue throughout summer. Serviceberry bushes grow in clearings and woods throughout the United States. Many Native Americans dried serviceberries to preserve them for future use. Sometimes they steamed the berries before drying them; other times they mashed or pounded them to form cakes, which were then dried. Pieces could be broken off these cakes as needed. Pemmican was made by pounding meat, animal fat, and berries together. These mild-flavored berries contain vitamin C.

Foods:
Tea: Fill a cup about 1/3 full with a combination of young shredded shoots, mashed dried berries, and dried leaves. Add boiling water. Cover and steep 10 to 20 minutes. Strain, sweeten, and serve.

Raw: Serviceberries can be eaten fresh off the vine or added to fruit salads, pancakes, muffins, breads, and cereals. They tend to vary in sweetness.

Cooked: They can also be cooked and used for pie fillings, jams, jellies, or fruit leathers.

Dried: Serviceberries can be dried like raisins.

SERVICEBERRY PANCAKES
(Serves 2)

> 3 eggs
> 1 1/4 cups flour
> 1/4 teaspoon salt
> 1 cup milk
> 2 tablespoons butter, melted
> 1/2 cup serviceberries, seeded
> 1/4 teaspoon vanilla
> 1/2 cup sugar
> Additional butter

Beat the eggs and stir in flour and salt. Blend in milk. Add butter, berries, vanilla, and sugar. Heat additional butter in a frying pan.

Pour the batter into the pan to form pancakes. The batter should be slightly runny. Lightly brown one side, flip and brown the other side. Serve hot with maple syrup and butter.

SHEPHERD'S PURSE

Capsella bursa-pastoris

St. James's Wort, Pepper and Salt, Mother's Heart

Features: Shepherd's purse, a small, erect, annual plant that grows 3 to 24 inches high, has an initial rosette of green dandelion-like leaves. A slightly branched stem rises from the center of these leaves. As it grows taller, widely spaced leaves grow along its length, diminishing in size as they approach the top. At the top of the stem, clusters of tiny white flowers appear. Later, green heart-shaped seedpods grow alternately along the stem and branches. Each seedpod has its own short stem. Peppergrass *(Lepidium virginicum)* is often confused with shepherd's purse. They're both about the same size, grow in similar environments, and have individual seedpods along their stems. However, peppergrass seedpods are oval, not heart-shaped. Both plants are edible and have a similar peppery flavor.

Facts: Shepherd's purse grows in lawns, waste places, and along roadsides throughout the United States. The leaves can be gathered during spring and summer, but the seeds are best when gathered in fall. Cahuilla Indians made a tea from shepherd's purse to cure dysentery, but it was considered unwise to drink more than 2 cups of this strong tea at a time. Because it's high in Vitamin K, shepherd's purse tea is also reputed to be effective in stopping internal bleeding and hemorrhaging. Two women, whom I know personally, drank this tea as a final resort in order to stop persistent bleeding. In both cases, it was effective.

Foods:

Tea: Put 1 teaspoon of bruised leaves into a cup. Fill with boiling water. Cover and steep for 5 minutes. Strain, sweeten and serve. Liquid left over from cooking the leaves can also be drunk.

Raw: Young lower leaves are mild and can be eaten as a snack or added to salads and sandwiches.

Cooked: They can be steamed, boiled, or stir-fried, and they mix well with other greens.

Seasoning: Shepherd's purse roots can be used fresh or dried as a substitute for ginger. As long as the plant is green, the roots are good. The seeds can be used fresh or dried as a substitute for pepper. Fresh seeds are spicier than the older, drier ones.

SOUR GRASS

Oxalis spp.

Features: Almost everyone recognizes the bright yellow flowers of sour grass—one of the first flowers to appear after winter rains. A single sour grass rootstock produces copious clusters of tall, slender, light green flower stems and leaf stems. Each flower stem is crowned by sunny bunches of 5-petaled yellow flowers. Clover-like leaves, comprised of 3 heart-shaped leaflets, grow singly atop the leaf stems. Many of these glowing green leaves are freckled with dark purplish-brown spots.

Facts: Sour grass grows in moist shady locations throughout the West and can be picked during spring and summer. Young plants always taste best. Oxalis contains oxalic acid which gives it its sour taste. Although oxalic acid is not harmful in small amounts, it can cause stomach upsets when consumed in large quantities. Some people claim that cooking will neutralize the oxalic acid, but others disagree. Surprisingly, cranberries, spinach and rhubarb also contain oxalic acid.

Foods:

Tea: Put 1/4 cup crushed leaves, flowers and stems into a cup. Add boiling water. Cover and steep for 5 minutes. Strain, sweeten and serve hot or cold.

Raw: All parts of sour grass are edible and can be eaten as a snack or added to salads and sandwiches.

SOUR GRASS COOLER
(Makes 1 quart)

> 1/2 - 1 cup sour grass leaves, stems and flowers
> 1 quart water or carbonated beverage
> Sugar or honey

Liquefy the sour grass and water or carbonated beverage in a blender. Sweeten to taste. Chill and serve. Because this attractive green cooler is sour, most people find it very refreshing.

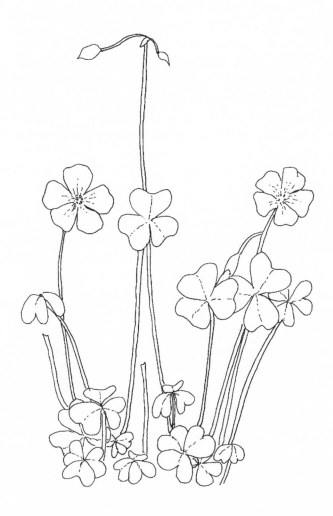

SOW THISTLE

Sonchus oleraceus

Features: Annual sow thistles first appear as low-growing rosettes of dandelion-like leaves which are sometimes reddish in color. A branched flower stem rises from the center of the rosette and the stem and branches are crowned with small dandelion-like flowers. Leaves growing along the stem are directly attached and appear to be hugging it. Sow thistle leaves are toothed, but not as prickly as those of prickly sow thistle. Its stems sometimes have purple splotches near their base. These hardy plants usually grow about knee high.

Facts: Sow thistles are available during most of the year and begin appearing by the end of winter. All parts are mild and tender when young. They can be found growing in waste places and moist areas throughout the United States. Actually, sow thistles are not thistles! They are members of the lettuce family and reputedly popular with pigs. *Sonchus oleraceus* is sometimes called "poison lettuce" because it has white sap, but there are no records of anyone being poisoned by it.

Foods:
Raw: The young leaves are mild and can be eaten after they are cleaned and the small prickles cut off. Peeled young stems are also tasty and add a pleasant crunchy texture to salads.

Cooked: Tender, new greens can be boiled, steamed, sautéed, or stir-fried. Young stems taste good steamed or boiled. First peel the stems, and cut them crosswise before cooking. Cook for about 10 minutes or until done. Serve with butter and salt.

ONE-POT PASTA
(Serves 4 – 6)

> Water
> 12 ounces spinach fettuccine
> 2 quarts sow thistle leaves, cleaned and chopped
> 1 pound mozzarella, grated
> 1/2 cup Parmesan
> Salt and pepper (optional)
> 2 cups tomatoes, diced

Boil water in a large pot. Cook pasta until tender. Drain, but retain 2 cups of liquid. Return the liquid to the pasta in the pot and heat to boiling. Add sow thistle greens. Cover and boil gently for 3 minutes more. Stir and add the mozzarella and Parmesan cheeses. Continue cooking and stirring until all cheese is melted. Season to taste with salt and pepper. Serve topped with tomatoes.

STINGING NETTLE

Urtica spp.

Features: Infamous stinging nettle is an erect, branched, perennial plant which grows 2 to 12 feet tall. All parts are covered with fine hairs which often cause temporary painful swellings upon contact. Dark green, heart-shaped leaves with saw-toothed margins grow opposite each other along the stems. Inconspicuous green flowers hang in clusters at the junctions of leaves and stems.

Facts: Stinging nettle thrives in moist locations throughout North America. Although some stinging nettle plants are available year-round, new plants usually appear during late winter or early spring and sometimes in fall. When gathering stinging nettle, avoid direct contact with your hands unless the plant is less than 6 inches tall. I use plastic bags to collect them. Stinging nettle contains more plant protein than any other plant and is also high in iron. Over the centuries this nutritious plant has been a welcome source of food, and its fibers have been used to make cloth and twine. Many people today wear sweaters made from ramie, not realizing that it is made from *Boehmeria nivea*, a plant related to stinging nettle.

Foods:
Tea: Put 1/2 cup of cleaned leaves into a cup. Add boiling water. Cover and steep for 5 minutes. Strain, sweeten and serve. You can also save and drink the liquid left over from cooking stinging nettle leaves. Cooked plants no longer sting on contact.

Cooked: Young leaves can be steamed or boiled. Five minutes is usually long enough, since overcooking makes them soggy. Because they are mild, stinging nettle greens mix well with stronger greens.

Dried: Stinging nettle leaves can be dried for future use as a seasoning, tea, or soup ingredient. Dried nettle doesn't sting.

NETTLE LASAGNA
(Serves 8 – 12)

8 ounces lasagna noodles
6 cups young stinging nettle greens, cleaned
1 egg, beaten
8 tablespoons Parmesan
15 ounces ricotta
12 ounces mozzarella, grated
32 ounces spaghetti sauce
Extra Parmesan

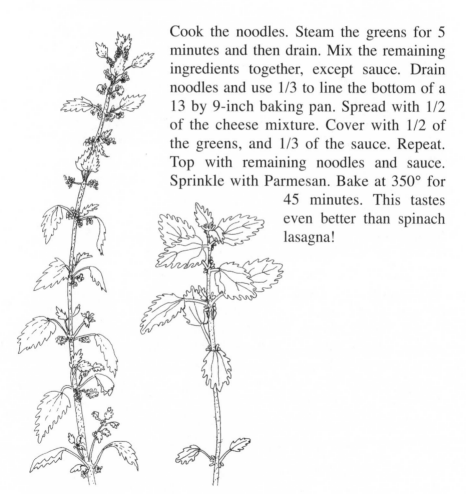

Cook the noodles. Steam the greens for 5 minutes and then drain. Mix the remaining ingredients together, except sauce. Drain noodles and use 1/3 to line the bottom of a 13 by 9-inch baking pan. Spread with 1/2 of the cheese mixture. Cover with 1/2 of the greens, and 1/3 of the sauce. Repeat. Top with remaining noodles and sauce. Sprinkle with Parmesan. Bake at 350° for 45 minutes. This tastes even better than spinach lasagna!

STORK'S BILL

Erodium cicutarium, E. moschatum

Filaree, Red-Stem Filaree, Scissors Plant

Features: Annual stork's bill is one of the earliest spring greens to appear. In Southern California it can often be spotted as early as February. At first glance its short, delicate, fern-like leaves appear to be a yellow-green shadow along the ground. But, by the time its 5-petaled, pale purple flowers appear, it's both taller and more conspicuous. Although the flower stalks can grow up to 1 1/2 feet tall, they're usually only a few inches high and grow in chaparral or desert habitats. The seedpods are long and narrow, becoming corkscrew-shaped when they mature, and often attach themselves to unwary passers-by. The flowers and seedpods of *E. cicutarium* grow in small clusters; whereas *E. moschatum*'s slightly larger flowers grow singly or in pairs, as do their seedpods, which are longer than those of *E. cicutarium*. Although some people may call stork's bill "heron's bill," the latter is actually a different but related plant. Heron's bill, *E. texanum,* has 3-lobed leaves, whereas stork's bill has fern-like leaves.

Facts: Stork's bill grows in open places throughout the West. The best time to gather it is spring. The Spanish name for stork's bill is "Alfilerea," which means "needle," and refers to its long, narrow, pointed seedpods. Another nickname given this prolific plant is "scissors plant," because a miniature pair of scissors can be made from 2 green seedpods. Just make a slit through the center of one seedpod and insert the other halfway through. With your help they will open and close just like real scissors.

Foods:
Raw: Young stork's bill can be nibbled raw on the trail or added to salads.

Cooked: It can be boiled, steamed, stir-fried, or added to soups.

STORK'S BILL OMELET
(Serves 2)

> 1 tablespoon butter
> 1/2 onion, minced
> 1 tomato, diced
> 1/2 cup stork's bill greens, cleaned and chopped
> 3 eggs, scrambled
> 1/4 - 1/2 cup cheddar cheese, grated
> Salt and pepper

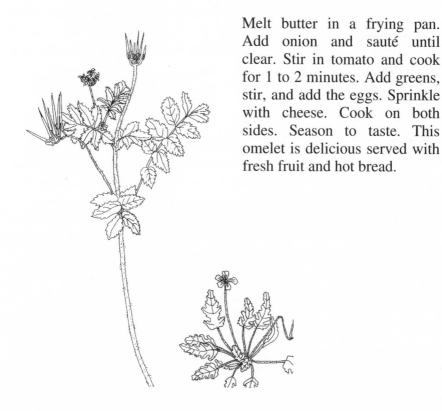

Melt butter in a frying pan. Add onion and sauté until clear. Stir in tomato and cook for 1 to 2 minutes. Add greens, stir, and add the eggs. Sprinkle with cheese. Cook on both sides. Season to taste. This omelet is delicious served with fresh fruit and hot bread.

STRAWBERRY

Fragaria vesca

Features: Growing only 2 to 6 inches high, small, lovely straw-berry plants nestle together under shady trees or near bushes. They spread by rhizomes and can usually be found in large low clusters covering the ground. A plant is comprised of several leaves and a few flowers, each leaf and flower on its own slender stem. All stems meet at the base of the plant. Each strawberry leaf is made up of three leaflets with sharply serrated margins. The stems and undersides of the leaves are covered with soft white hairs. Tiny strawberry flowers, each with 5 white petals and yellow centers, grow in small clusters. The berries that follow are first green, then white, and finally red and juicy when ripe.

Facts: Strawberry plants grow in open woodlands throughout the United States. Leaves can be gathered during spring and summer. Strawberries usually mature between May and early July. Both the leaves and berries are high in vitamin C. Mashed strawberries are said to be soothing to sunburns and helpful in removing tartar when rubbed on teeth.

Foods:
Tea: Tea can be made from dried or fresh leaves. (Never use wilted leaves). Put 3 to 6 crushed leaves into a cup. Fill with boiling water. Cover and steep for 5 minutes. Strain, sweeten and serve. This tea is reputed to be an aid in healing soft gums and loose teeth.

Raw: Both fruit and leaves can be eaten raw or added to salads. Strawberries are especially good served in desserts and smoothies.

Cooked: All parts can be steamed, boiled, or added to soups and stews.

SENSATIONAL STRAWBERRY SHERBET
(Serves 2)

>1 cup buttermilk
>1 cup strawberries, cleaned
>1/2 cup sugar
>1/2 teaspoon vanilla

Blend all ingredients together in blender. Pour into a freezer dish. Freeze until firm, then refrigerate 1/2 hour before serving.

STRAWBERRY SMOOTHIE
(Serves 1)

>1 cup orange juice
>1 banana
>1/4 - 1/2 cup strawberries
>4 ice cubes

Blend juice and fruit together in blender. Add ice cubes one at a time. The result is a delicious, refreshing drink high in vitamin C and potassium.

SWEET FENNEL

Foeniculum vulgare

Features: Perennial sweet fennel is a delicate, bushy plant which grows 3 to 6 feet tall. In spring, young fennel is a yellowish-green cluster of feathery fern-like leaves. Thick like bamboo, a branched flower stalk rises from the center of this leaf cluster. Small yellow flowers grow in double umbels at the top of stalk and branches. New smaller leaves appear along the flower stalk. Later, the flowers mature into numerous small green seeds which become brown as they age. All parts of sweet fennel smell like licorice when bruised. This plant is often confused with anise *(Pimpinella anisum)* because of their similar flavor, but they don't look alike! Anise is much sorter and has white flowers. Sweet fennel is also sometimes mistaken for poison hemlock *(Conium maculatum)*. However, poison hemlock has brownish-purple spots on its flower stalks, its leaves are different, and it does not have a licorice smell when bruised. Poison hemlock leaves are fern-like; whereas sweet fennel leaves are thread-like.

Facts: Originally from Europe, sweet fennel grows in vacant lots, along streams, and in other moist places—especially along the Pacific Coast and throughout California. In southern California the young leaves appear as early as February. Fresh sweet fennel leaves always taste good, but plant bases taste best when picked before the flowers bloom. Fennel seeds are usually available by summer. They are easily dried, and can be stored for future use.

Foods:
Tea: Put 1/2 teaspoon of clean fennel seeds or some young leaves into a mug. Fill with boiling water. Cover and steep for 5 minutes. Strain and serve. Fennel tea is said to be slightly diuretic.

Raw: Young stalks, leaves, and seeds can all be eaten as a snack or added to salads. They have a sweet flavor and freshen your breath.

Cooked: Young stalks, before they flower, can be steamed, boiled, or sautéed. They taste good served with regular melted butter, or orange-flavored melted butter.

JUDITH'S THREE WEEK HONEY CAKE
(Makes 1 loaf)

> 1 cup honey
> 1 cup brown sugar
> 1 cup low-fat or non-fat milk
> 3 cups flour
> 1 teaspoon allspice
> 1 teaspoon fennel seeds
> 2 teaspoons baking powder

Mix honey, sugar and milk together. In a separate bowl combine the other ingredients. Then gradually add them into the honey mixture, using an electric beater. Pour into a greased loaf pan and bake at 350° for 1 hour or until done. This delicious, low-cholesterol cake stays fresh for several weeks; if you don't eat it first! It's great for camping, hiking and picnics.

THIMBLEBERRY

Rubus parviflorus

Features: Thimbleberry shrubs are deciduous, spread outward and grow 3 to 6 feet tall. Their soft hairy leaves are large, growing from 4 to 7 inches wide. Striking, large, white flowers, up to 2 inches across, cluster in bunches of 2 or 3 at the end of some of the branches. Dull red, lumpy thimbleberries resemble raspberries in size and appearance. They're hollow and open at the bottom like a thimble. New growth is slightly reddish, turning brown as it ages.

Facts: These bushes favor both moist and dry fields, and woods at higher elevations throughout the United States. The berries are fully ripe by late summer. Both bark and leaves of thimbleberry shrubs have medicinal uses; they can be used as an astringent or boiled to produce a steam which is said to be good for oily skin. Thimbleberries were an important food for northwestern Native Americans, who ate them raw or dried. Cakes formed from dried berries keep well. Pieces of the cakes were chipped off as needed and added to soups.

Foods:
Tea: Put part of a dried leaf or a few inches of young twigs into a cup. Fill with boiling water. Cover and steep for 10 minutes. Strain and serve.

Raw: Thimbleberries can be eaten right off the bush. They have a delicate, pleasant flavor. Young tender shoots, which usually appear during spring, can be eaten raw.

Cooked: Young shoots can be sautéed or stir-fried.

BERRY GOOD JELL-O

(Serves 4 – 6)

  3 ounces raspberry Jell-O
  1 cup boiling water
  1 cup sour cream

Mix Jell-O and boiling water together. Blend in sour cream. Refrigerate in a large bowl or mold for about 4 hours or until firm.

  3 ounces raspberry Jell-O
  1 cup boiling water
  1 cup cold water
  1 cup thimbleberries
  1/4 cup walnuts, chopped

Mix Jell-O and boiling water together. Then add cold water. Stir in berries and walnuts. Cool for 5-10 minutes, and then pour on top of the firm mixture. Return the mold to the refrigerator for about 4 hours or until set.

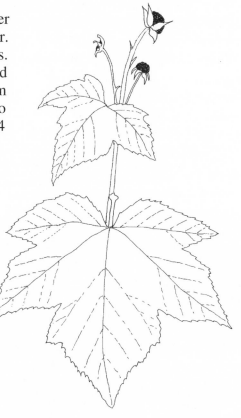

THISTLE

Cirsium spp.

Features: There are many varieties of thistles—all edible. Some are annuals and some are perennials. Thistles are easily recognized by their size and the numerous spines which grow along leaf margins and stalks. Their leaves usually grow directly from stiff stalks, and are deeply lobed with sharp points and stiff spines at their tips. Blue, purple, red, pink, yellow or white thistle flower heads are actually bunches of long tubular flowers that have no petals. The two thistles illustrated; bull thistle *(C. vulgare)*, and wild artichoke *(Cynera cardunculus)*, both have purple flowers. Bull thistle flowers are red-violet in color, and wild artichoke flowers are a vivid blue-violet. Wild artichokes are very conspicuous, often towering overhead at heights of 8 feet or more; whereas bull thistles generally only grow to be 1 1/2 to 3 feet tall.

Facts: Thistles grow in most environments throughout the United States and are available from late winter through fall. They're very useful plants. Their stems contain fibers which can be twisted into twine and their down can be used to help start fires. Old records indicate that in 1870, a botanist named Truman Everts got lost while exploring Yellowstone National Park. Even though he broke his glasses and had trouble seeing, he managed to survive for over a month just by eating elk thistle roots, which he could identify by touch.

Foods:
Raw: Young thistle leaves tend to be bitter, but they can be eaten raw or added to salads and sandwiches after their spines have been cut off. Young roots can also be eaten raw.

Cooked: These young roots are surprisingly good when sliced crosswise and boiled for about 20 minutes or until tender. Young peeled stems can be bundled like asparagus and boiled. They taste good served hot with butter, or served cold in a salad with tomatoes, parsley, green onions and dressing. Unopened buds, especially from wild artichokes, can be boiled and eaten like artichokes. Their hearts can be scooped out and served with sauce. Average sized buds take about 20 minutes to cook. Buds are usually available from late spring until late summer.

BOILED THISTLE ROOT WITH CHEESE SAUCE
(Serves 2 – 4)

> 1 cup thistle roots, peeled and sliced
> 1/2 cup water

Boil for about 35 minutes until no longer bitter, or boil in 2 changes of water. Drain.

CHEESE SAUCE

> 1 1/2 tablespoons butter
> 2 tablespoons flour
> 3/4 cup milk
> 1 ounce sharp cheddar cheese

Melt butter, slowly add flour, and gradually add milk and cheese, stirring constantly. Lower the heat and continue stirring until cheese is melted and sauce is thick. Serve over boiled thistle roots.

Bull Thistle   Wild Artichoke

TOYON

Heteromeles arbutifolia

Christmas Berry, California Holly

Features: Toyons are large evergreen shrubs or small trees which can reach heights of 30 feet. Leathery, dark green, toothed leaves grow alternately along branches. Small, white, 5-petaled flowers grow in loose compound clusters, to be replaced by numerous, bright red, pea-sized berries.

Facts: Toyons can be found growing on dry ground at lower elevations throughout California. The berries don't mature until fall. It's commonly believed that Hollywood got its name from the profusion of holly-like toyons which grow on hills there. Because red toyon berries mature around Christmas time, they are also called "Christmas berries." Both Spaniards and Native Americans ate cooked toyon berries. Sometimes they roasted them in a fire before cooking to remove their slightly bitter flavor.

Foods:
Tea: Although tea can be made from the bark, it is less harmful to the tree if you use the leaves. They can be picked at any time during the year. Put a few leaves into a cup. Fill with boiling water. Cover and steep for 5 to 10 minutes. Strain and serve. Or, boil 1 tablespoon ripe berries in 1 cup of water for a few minutes for a mild tea which is reputedly a cure for stomachache.

Raw: Toyon berries can be eaten raw, but are dry and not very tasty.

Cooked: They can be toasted, steamed, or boiled, and taste best if you add sugar. Native Americans boiled the berries and then roasted them underground for 2 to 3 days. Nowadays, they can be sprinkled with sugar, tied up in cheesecloth, and roasted in a slow oven or steamed for several hours.

TUMBLEWEED

Salsola kali

Russian Thistle

Features: When we think of tumbleweed we usually picture a 1 to 2 1/2 foot tall brittle ball of bare branches tumbling madly along the ground. But this is only Russian thistle in its final stages. Young tumbleweed is a small, tender, green, annual plant with soft flexible spines. The larger, more mature plants have lovely, inconspicuous, greenish-white flowers which often have delicate red centers. These flowers grow along stems and branches.

Facts: Tumbleweeds grow in disturbed places around the world. Although they are evident during much of the year, the young plants are only available from spring until fall. *Salsola kali* originally came from Europe, but Native Americans soon developed many ways to prepare it. For a time, in Europe, a form of carbonate of soda called "barilla" was made from tumbleweed ashes.

Foods:
Raw: Very young tumbleweed can be chopped and eaten in salads. Young tender plants often appear as early as late winter, and new growth can be gathered throughout spring. By summer the plants are usually too brittle to eat raw.

Cooked: New growth, (under 10 inches), and tender tips of older plants can be steamed, boiled, sautéed, or added to soups and stews. Young greens are also good in omelets. Mild-flavored tumbleweed mixes well with other greens.

CREAMED TUMBLEWEED OVER BISCUITS
(Serves 2)

> 6 biscuits
> 1 cup tumbleweed greens, chopped
> 1 tablespoon butter
> 2 tablespoons flour
> 1 cup milk
> 1 pinch basil
> Salt and pepper

Bake or heat the biscuits. Meanwhile, steam tumbleweed 5 to 10 minutes, and prepare sauce. Melt butter and slowly stir in flour. Gradually add milk. Lower heat and continue stirring until thickened. Season with basil, salt and pepper. Drain tumbleweed and add to sauce. Slice biscuits in half and smother with sauce. Serve immediately.

TUMBLEWEED SOUFFLÉ
(Serves 2)

> 1 cup water
> 2 cups tender tumbleweed leaves
> 2 cups lamb's quarters leaves (see page 62)
> 1 cup béchamel sauce (see page 55)
> 1/2 cup cheddar cheese, grated
> 2 eggs, beaten
> Parmesan

Boil water and add greens. Cover and boil gently for 5 minutes. Meanwhile, prepare the béchamel sauce and add cheddar cheese. Drain the greens. Combine all ingredients except Parmesan, and put into a greased baking pan. Sprinkle with Parmesan and bake at 325° until lightly browned—about 20 to 25 minutes.

VERONICA

Veronica aquatica

Water Speedwell, Brooklime

Features: Veronica is a semi-aquatic perennial herb which thrives in shallow water or damp places. It grows from 6 inches to 3 feet in height. Narrow, green, pointed, slightly-toothed leaves grow in alternate pairs up fragile slender stalks. Small flower stems grow above the leaf joints along the main stalk. Tiny leaves and pale lavender flowers with 4 irregular petals adorn the upper section of the flower stems. Veronica can usually be found hidden among cattails, bulrushes, and mints.

Facts: This plant grows in shallow water or other moist locations throughout the West. Young leaves are available from spring through summer. All species of veronica are edible and contain large quantities of vitamin C. This is why veronica was formerly used to prevent scurvy and to make cough syrups and skin salves. In Japan and Europe, veronica is considered a delicacy. Because it grows in or near water, always be sure that the water source is clean, or disinfect the plants before eating them.

Foods:
Tea: Fill a cup 1/4 full with clean stems and leaves. Fill with boiling water. Cover and steep for 5 minutes. Strain and serve.

Raw: Fresh leaves and stems are pleasantly mild and can be added to salads and sandwiches.

Cooked: They can also be steamed or added to soups but are best eaten raw because they shrink down when cooked.

RICE VERONICA

(Serves 2)

> 1 tablespoon olive oil
> 1 clove garlic
> 1/2 onion, chopped
> 1 cup veronica greens, cleaned and chopped
> 1/3 cup peas
> 1/2 cup white rice, uncooked
> 1 1/4 cups water
> 1 tablespoon soy sauce
> Salt

Heat olive oil. Sauté garlic and onion until clear. Stir in greens, peas, and rice. Add water. Cover and bring to a boil, then lower heat and simmer for about 20 minutes or until all liquid is absorbed. Add soy sauce and salt.

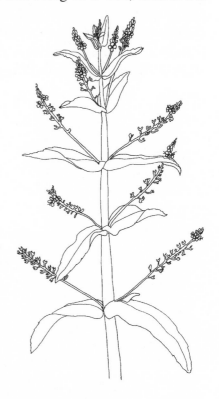

WATERCRESS

Nasturtium officinale

Features: Watercress is a common aquatic perennial herb. Adorned with shiny compound leaves that glow in the sunshine, hollow stems and branches of watercress grow up through water, secured by their roots. The stems are usually 6 to 18 inches long and extend 2 to 4 inches above the water's surface. Tiny, 4-petaled, white watercress flowers grow in tight terminal clusters. If only the tips are gathered, the plants will continue to produce new growth.

Facts: Watercress is often seen growing in streams and drainage ditches throughout the West. Young watercress is available from spring through summer. Because *Nasturtium officinale* is high in vitamin C, many people, including Greeks, Romans, Persians and Native Americans have valued its health promoting properties. Watercress is also reputed to be a cure for liver and kidney illnesses, gallstones, and even mental problems.

Foods:
Raw: Spicy watercress can be eaten as a snack or added to salads and sandwiches, especially cream cheese or butter sandwiches. Because it often grows in water of questionable purity, extra care should be taken in cleaning wild watercress. One method is to soak it for several minutes in a solution made up of 4 drops of Clorox dissolved in 2 quarts of water.

Cooked: Watercress is excellent boiled, steamed, or stir-fried. It has a peppery flavor and mixes well with milder greens.

WONDERFUL WATERCRESS SOUP
(Serves 4 – 6)

> 2 tablespoons butter
> 2 cloves garlic, minced
> 1 onion, diced
> 2 cups watercress greens, cleaned and chopped
> 4 cups broth or water
> 4 potatoes, diced
> 4 cups milk
> 1 teaspoon salt
> 1/4 teaspoon pepper
> 1 teaspoon thyme

Melt butter in a large pot and sauté garlic and onion until clear. Stir in greens. Cover and cook until limp. Add broth or water and cover. When it begins to boil, add potatoes. Cover and cook 10 minutes more. Lower heat and stir in milk, salt, pepper and thyme. Heat until warm, but don't boil. This soup is excellent served with hot, crusty, sourdough bread.

MEDITERRANEAN WATERCRESS SALAD
(Serves 2 – 4)

> 1 cucumber, diced
> 4 tomatoes, diced
> 1 onion, minced
> 2 cups watercress, chopped
> 2 ounces feta, crumbled
> 2 tablespoons lemon juice
> 2 tablespoons olive oil
> Salt and pepper

Combine all ingredients. Season to taste with salt and pepper.

WHITE SAGE

Salvia apiana

Features: White sage is a striking, aromatic shrub which grows 3 to 6 feet tall. Pale gray-green in color, it appears almost white in contrast to neighboring plants. Young leaves of white sage are crowded and opposite. Tall, erect, flower stalks appear early in spring. Small, pale lavender to white flowers grow in tiered whorls along the stems from April to June. Large leaves cluster around the base of the flower stalk.

Facts: Prolific white sage grows in coastal sage scrub communities and in dry waste places throughout the West and elsewhere. The best time to gather it is from April to June. Because white sage has such a strong odor, it has many uses. Today, as in the past, many Native Americans burn it in their sweat lodges for purification. They gather small bundles of leaves, dry them, and light their tips to create a pleasant-smelling smudge that is used in rituals. It is said that when Kumeyaay hunters went out to hunt, they sometimes carried white sage under their arms to disguise their human scent.

Foods:
Tea: White sage makes a delicious tea that is reputedly good for your digestion. Put only a portion of 1 leaf into a cup. Add boiling water. Cover and steep for 5 minutes. Strain, sweeten and serve. This tea has also been used as a wash for infections. It's said to be calming to nerves and an aid in digesting heavy meals.

Raw: Young shoots can be eaten raw, but they have a very strong flavor.

Cooked: Native Americans sometimes gathered, parched, and ground white sage seeds to make a meal which was cooked as mush. The seeds were also used for flavoring.

LEMON SAGE TEA
(Makes 1 quart)

> 4 small white sage leaves, bruised
> 2 tablespoons sugar
> Juice of 1 lemon
> 1 teaspoon grated lemon rind
> 1 quart boiling water

Put sage leaves, sugar, lemon juice and lemon rind into a pitcher. Add boiling water. Cover and steep for 5 minutes. Strain and serve hot or cold.

WILD CELERY

Apium graveolens

Smallage

Features: Biennial wild celery has erect ribbed stems which grow 1 to 3 feet tall. Its deeply 3-lobed, slightly toothed, light green leaves become darker in color during their second year. Small white flowers, arranged in umbels, grow along the branches and at their tips. These graceful plants are very prolific, especially in shallow stream beds. Some people confuse poison hemlock with wild celery because they resemble each other somewhat and grow in similar environments. There are three major differences: wild celery has fuller rounder lobes on its leaves than poison hemlock, wild celery has no purple splotches on its stems but poison hemlock does, and finally, wild celery has a pleasant, distinctive odor when crushed, whereas crushed poison hemlock smells slightly unpleasant.

Facts: Wild celery thrives in moist nonalkaline locations such as coastal sage scrub and chaparral areas near streams. Young plants first appear in spring and are found in California from San Diego north to Sacramento County west of the Sierras. Wild celery is high in calcium, phosphorus, iron, and vitamin A and was eaten for its nutritional value by such ancient people as the Greeks and Romans.

Foods:
Tea: Fill a cup 1/3 full with cleaned wild celery leaves. Add boiling water. Cover and steep for 5 minutes. Strain and serve. Wild celery tea is said to be good for indigestion and kidney complaints.

Raw: Wild celery is stronger than the domestic variety but it can be added in moderation to salads and sandwiches or filled with peanut butter and cream cheese.

Cooked: Stalks and leaves can be steamed, boiled, sautéed, or added to soups and stews. Wild celery goes well with cream sauces.

SUCCULENT CELERY SOUP
(Serves 4)

4 tablespoons butter
2 onions, diced
4 cloves garlic, minced
2 cups wild celery, sliced
4 potatoes, diced
2 cups water
4 cups milk
Juice of 1/2 lemon
Salt and pepper
Several celery leaves
Sour cream (optional)

Melt butter. Sauté onion and garlic until clear. Stir in celery and potatoes. Add water and cover. Bring to a boil, then lower heat and simmer at least 10 minutes. Add milk and heat, but don't boil. Add lemon juice and season with salt and pepper to taste. Cool slightly, and then blend in a blender until smooth. Reheat before serving. Garnish with celery leaves and possibly a dollop of sour cream.

WILD GRAPES

Vitis californica

Features: Perennial wild grapes grow on woody vines. Their large heart-shaped leaves are deeply lobed and have sharply saw-toothed margins. Green grapes hang in bunches, becoming purple with a dusting of white when ripe. There are many different varieties of edible wild grapes. *V. californica* has  small yellow flowers which usually bloom from May to June. Young tendrils are available during spring and sparingly in summer.

Facts: Wild grapes grow in stream beds and canyons below 4,000 feet in southern Canada and throughout the United States. The grapes aren't ready to pick until late summer, but the leaves need to be picked earlier while they are still young and tender. Because grapes are high in iron and potassium, grape juice is often recommended to treat anemia. Grape sugar is easily digested and wine is said to be good for the digestion. Several studies indicate that drinking one glass of red wine daily helps to prevent heart attacks.

Foods:
Tea: Leftover liquid from cooked grape leaves can be drunk as tea, or a crushed leaf can be steeped in 1 cup of boiling water for 5 minutes.

Raw: Grapes can be eaten right off the vine. Young leaves and tendrils can also be eaten raw as a snack. The tendrils have a refreshing lemony flavor and a pleasant crunchy texture.

Cooked: Grapes can be made into jams, jellies, juices, syrup, or wine. Grape leaves can be boiled, steamed, sautéed, or stuffed.

Dried: When grapes are dried they become raisins.

STUFFED GRAPE LEAVES
(Serves 4)

24 grape leaves (6 inches across)
3 cups water

Trim stems off leaves. Add leaves to boiling water and boil for 5 minutes. Rinse under cold water. Line a large oven-proof frying pan with 4 leaves. Set the others aside.

STUFFING

1 large onion, chopped
1/4 cup rice, uncooked
1/3 cup fresh parsley, chopped
4 fresh mint leaves, chopped
2 tablespoons pine nuts
2 tablespoons raisins or currants
1/4 cup olive oil
1/8 teaspoon salt
1 lemon, sliced
2 cups water

Mix all ingredients together except lemon slices and water. Place grape leaves with the stem end facing you. Put one small tbs. of stuffing near the stem end. Roll this end over the stuffing. Fold in the sides and continue rolling until the finished grape leaf resembles a small cigar. Arrange them side by side in the frying pan. When all 20 are in the pan, top with a layer of thin lemon slices. Pour 2 cups of water over all. Cover tightly with a lid or ovenproof plate and bake at 350° for 1 1/2 hours. Serve cold with fresh lemon slices. Sprinkle with additional lemon juice if desired.

WILD RADISH

Raphanus sativus

Features: Bushy wild radish is a hardy, prolific, annual or biannual plant which can grow over 4 feet tall. Its stiff, slender, green stem and branches often become purplish-brown as they mature. The initial, basal, deeply-cut leaves are larger and more divided than the following leaves, which diminish in size and complexity as they grow along stem and branches. All wild radish leaves have toothed margins and are covered with fine hairs which can be felt if you touch them. At the tips of the branches are small clusters of yellow, white, rose or lilac colored cruciferous flowers, with 4 tiny paddle-like petals arranged in the shape of a cross. These flowers aren't replaced by seeds. Seedpods, which are often evident simultaneously with the flowers, appear along the branches. These numerous, stiff, slender seedpods, each on its own stem, are irregularly arranged and point rigidly upward. Yellow-flowering wild radish greatly resembles black mustard, but there are subtle differences. Wild radish flowers are slightly larger, and there are fewer per cluster. Its seedpods are also larger than those of black mustard. Both plants are edible.

Facts: Wild radishes grow in waste places in Europe as well as throughout the United States. These plants are available from February until July.

Foods:
Raw: Leaves, flowers and seeds, which all have a spicy, radish-like flavor, can be eaten as a snack or added to salads and sandwiches. Wild radish roots are too strongly flavored to be eaten.

Cooked: Young leaves can be boiled, or added in moderation to soups and stews as seasoning.

WILD RADISH SALAD
(Serves 4)

    4 cups lettuce, torn
    1 green pepper, diced
    2 stalks celery, sliced
    2 scallions, minced
    2 teaspoons green wild radish seedpods, minced
    1/2 cucumber, diced
    4 tablespoons lemon juice
    2 tablespoons water
    3 tablespoons sugar

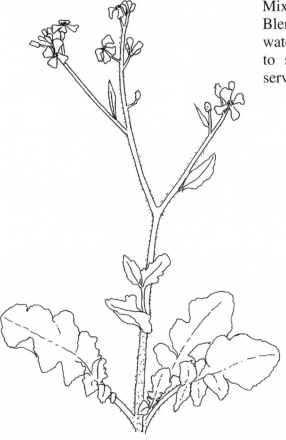

Mix vegetables together. Blend lemon juice and water with sugar and add to salad. Mix well and serve.

WILD ROSE

Rosa californica

Prickly Rose

Features: There are over 100 varieties of wild roses in the United States alone! All are edible. Branched, sprawling, wild rose shrubs grow 3 to 8 feet tall. Their compound leaves are made up of 5 to 7 narrow, oval leaflets with toothed margins. Rose or pink-colored 5-petaled flowers grow singly or in small clusters. Wild rose fruit, called "hips" or "rosehips," become orange or red when ripe, depending upon the variety. Rosehips, which mature during summer, remain on the bushes throughout winter, providing food for animals. Rosehips taste sweetest when gathered after the first frost.

Facts: Worldwide, wild roses grow best in moist locations. Their leaves are available year-round, the flowers are most evident during spring and summer, and fresh rosehips are available from summer through winter. Rosehips are extremely high in vitamin C, and their skins are high in vitamin E. Consequently, they were often used as a remedy for scurvy. Even after they are dried, they can be rehydrated and eaten. Czechoslovakians often cut the rosehips in half, remove the seeds, and then use the hips fresh or dried to make tea during winter.

Foods:
Tea: Crumble 3 to 4 leaves and place into a cup. Add boiling water. Cover and steep for 5 minutes. Strain, sweeten and serve. For rosehip tea; put 4 tablespoons of dried rosehips into a cup. Fill with boiling water, cover and steep for 5 minutes. Drain the water, crush the hips, and fill again with boiling water. Cover and steep for 5 minutes more. Then strain out the rosehips, sweeten the remaining liquid, and serve.

Raw: Rose hips can be eaten raw after they are cut open and the hairy seeds inside removed. Young peeled wild rose shoots can also be eaten raw.

Cooked: During spring and early summer, new leaves and flowers can be steamed, boiled, or sautéed. The remaining liquid can be drunk. Rosehips can be made into jams, jellies, or drinks, but don't use aluminum or copper pots because they destroy vitamin C.

A HIP DRINK
(Makes 1 quart)

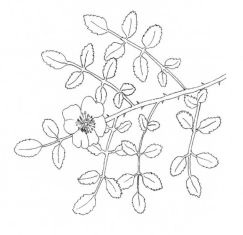

1 cup firm, ripe rosehips
1 quart water
Sugar or honey

Clean and crush rosehips. Place them into a pitcher, cover with water and soak overnight. In the morning, strain out the rosehips. Sweeten the remaining liquid and chill.

ROSEHIP JAM
(Makes 1 pint)

2 cups sugar
1 cup water
2 cups firm ripe rosehips, halved and seeded
2 tart apples, diced
4 tablespoons lemon juice
1 package pectin

Boil sugar and water gently for 4 minutes. Add the other ingredients. Cover and boil over low heat for 15 minutes, stirring occasionally. Then cook at a rolling boil for 2 minutes Pour into sterilized containers and seal or freeze.

WILLOW

Salix spp.

Features: There are 200-300 varieties of willow that grow throughout the world, ranging in size from only a few inches to trees up to 30 feet tall. Willows are characterized by their long, narrow, lance-shaped leaves that are four times as long as they are wide. These leaves are green above and so pale beneath as to appear silver or white in sunlight. New growth is slender, and surprisingly flexible—a reason why willow is often used to make baskets or furniture. Willows are also known for their soft, fuzzy, gray, upright catkins which are called "pussy willows." Mule fat *(Baccharis glutinosa)*, which also grows along streams, is often mistaken for willow. The best way to tell them apart is to look at the underside of their leaves. Mule fat leaves are the same color on both sides; whereas willow leaves are significantly paler beneath. Their flowers are also different. White to cream-colored mule fat flowers grow in clusters, whereas yellow-green willow flowers grow along flower stalks in drooping catkins. They also smell different. Only willow has a pleasant dried plant scent.

Facts: Most species of willows are found growing in or near shallow water, especially riverbeds. Willow leaves can be gathered at any time of the year. They contain salicin, which becomes salicylic acid—the main ingredient of aspirin. Native Americans chewed on willow stems and bark, or drank willow tea to relieve pain. Settlers followed their example. More recently, this acid was identified and synthetically developed for medicinal purposes. Bark, stems, and leaves can still be used to fight pain. But, just as with aspirin, it is better to take too little than too much. Willow also contains a large quantity of vitamin C, up to 7 to 10 times more than oranges.

Foods:

Tea: It's hard to know how much "aspirin" you're getting in your cup of tea, so it's best to use willow sparingly. Put part of 1 leaf into a cup. Add boiling water. Cover and steep for 5 to 10 minutes. Willow tea is said to be beneficial for headaches and arthritis. Don't try this tea if you are allergic to aspirin or are using an anticoagulant.

Raw: Some say that you can chew on the inner bark or new growth to get relief from fever, stomachaches, and headaches. Young leaves, buds, new sprouts, and inner bark can all be eaten as survival food. But bark should only be eaten in an emergency in order to avoid harming the tree.

WOOLY BLUE CURLS

Trichostema spp.

Blue Curls, Vinegar-Weed, Camphor Weed

Features: You can smell wooly blue curls even before you see them. They are nondescript, dusty, bushy, little plants which often go unnoticed. Only the small, intensely blue-violet flowers, with their scorpion-like curled stamens, stand out. Blue curls' square, brittle stems are either upright or prostrate, with numerous branches rising vertically in graceful arcs. The perennial varieties, shrubs that grow 2 to 4 feet high, may have woody stems, but the annual blue curls are tender plants growing only 3 to 16 inches high. Their soft, woolly, lance-shaped leaves are pointed and grow in pairs along three sides of the branches, not all the way around. Both stems and leaves are a pale, faded green. Flowers grow along the fourth side of the branches where there are no leaves. These irregular flowers have three petals which hang down in front, one diagonal petal on each side, one inconspicuous petal on top, and four hair-like stamens which curl upward and backward over the rest of the flower. Wooly blue curls are available during summer and early fall.

Facts: They can be found growing on hills and mountains of California, Arizona, and New Mexico. Some Mexicans call this plant *romero* because its leaves resemble those of rosemary, which they also call *romero*. Native Americans mashed these strongly scented leaves and threw them into shallow water to stupefy fish. Chumash Indians gave new mothers a tea made from blue curls leaves to help expel afterbirth. These leaves have also been used to make a liniment for bruises.

Foods:

USE IN MODERATION.

Tea: A little wooly blue curls goes a long way. So, for tea put only a few flowers and 1 of the upper leaves into a cup. Add boiling water. Cover and steep for 10 minutes. Strain, sweeten, and serve. This refreshing tea is said to help with colds, ague, and general disability. It tastes less bitter if you include flowers with the leaves.

YARROW

Achillea spp.

Milfoil

Features: Yarrow is a pale perennial which grows 1 to 3 feet high. Its stiff, almost branchless stem grows upright and is crowned with a flat cluster of tiny, white, pink, or reddish flowers. Delicate, pale green, fern-like leaves grow alternately along the stem, decreasing in size as they approach the top. They emit a pleasant odor when crushed. Before the stem appears, young yarrow plants consist of small clusters of fragile, feathery, upright leaves joined together at their base. It's always best to gather the young plants in spring.

Facts: Yarrow is found in dry forests and chaparral throughout the West and in similar environments elsewhere. It is considered by many to have medicinal properties. Native Americans drank a tea made from the whole plant as a tonic. Yarrow steam was used to clear their sinuses. In Europe, Roman soldiers crushed the entire plant and used it on wounds to staunch the flow of blood. A drink made from yarrow is said to be good for fevers and headaches. However, because yarrow contains some alkaloid poison, it should be used in moderation despite its healing properties. Its nickname, "milfoil," is French and means one thousand leaves. This is a good name for yarrow because each of its fern-like leaves is divided and redivided, making it appear to have many leaves. Its Latin name, Achillea, is said to refer to Achilles of Greek mythology, who crushed this plant and used it to staunch the flow of blood from his wounded heel. Today we often refer to a person's weakness as his "Achilles' heel."

Foods:

USE IN MODERATION.

Tea: Put 2 to 3 fresh leaves or 1/2 teaspoon of dried plant into a cup. Add boiling water. Cover and steep for 10 minutes. Strain, sweeten, and serve. If this is too strong for your taste, only steep the tea for 5 minutes or use fewer leaves. Yarrow tea is recommended for run-down conditions.

Raw: A few chopped leaves can be added to cream cheese sandwiches.

Dried: Yarrow leaves can be ground up and used as a substitute for pepper.

YERBA MANSA

Anemopsis californica

Features: Yerba mansa, a perennial herb, grows 6 to 24 inches high and spreads by rhizomes. Its initial leaves are ovate in shape and form a rosette. Each leaf grows on a separate stem, joining the other stems just above the surface of the ground. In spring, cone-shaped flowers appear, surrounded by 6 to 7 white petal-like bracts. Sometimes there are smaller leaves growing along the hollow flower stalks or even encircling them. After the flowers dry up, reddish or brown blotches often appear on the leaves. Both leaves and rootstocks are very aromatic.

Facts: Yerba mansa thrives in wet alkaline places throughout the Southwest. The roots can be gathered all year but are most potent after the leaves have died back in fall and winter. Yerba mansa's

name derives from *yerba del manso*. This literally means "herb of the tame," and refers to Native Americans who worked at missions and used yerba mansa. Yerba mansa was considered a good cure for many different ailments.

Foods:
Tea: Tea can be brewed from fresh or dried roots. Boil a small piece of root for several minutes. Strain, sweeten and serve. Internally, this tea is said to be good for indigestion, asthma, and impure blood. Externally, it can be applied to skin diseases, cuts, bruises and sores. It has a pleasant refreshing mint flavor and a wonderful aroma.

Raw: Fresh or dried roots can be chewed to relieve thirst and sore throats, or just because they taste good.

Cooked: Heated leaves are sometimes used as a poultice for swellings. Liquid from boiled leaves can be added to bath water to soothe and relax sore muscles or it can be added to basins of warm water to soak sore feet.

YERBA SANTA

Eriodictyon californicum

Thick-Leafed Yerba Santa

Features: Thick-leafed yerba santa is a lovely aromatic evergreen shrub which grows from 2 to 8 feet tall. Its thick, woolly, pale gray-green leaves grow alternately along stems and branches. These leaves are long and narrow, and usually have toothed margins. As the plant grows taller, new leaves, decreasing in size, grow more widely spaced than the older ones. Sometimes, as early as February, small clusters of pale lavender-white flowers appear on the ends of branches.

Facts: Yerba santa grows in dry open places from Oregon to southern California. Yerba santa means "holy herb" in Spanish. Although it makes a tasty tea, this herb is much better known for its medicinal properties. The leaves are said to be their most potent when they are stickiest. This usually occurs in late spring or after abundant showers. Yerba santa tea is recommended for coughs, colds, sore throats and asthma. The leaves can be crushed and used as a poultice or smoked as tobacco. As with yerba mansa, yerba santa was considered a "cure-all" for most medical problems by many Native Americans.

Foods:
Tea: Crush 2 leaves and place into a cup. Add boiling water. Cover and steep for 5 minutes. Strain and sweeten with sugar or honey.

Raw: You can chew on a fresh leaf to freshen your mouth and alleviate thirst. Initially, it may taste bitter. The flavor is said to improve after the first few minutes. I've tried chewing on them, but they always taste bitter to me...

YUCCA

Yucca schidigera, Yucca whipplei

Spanish Bayonet, Our Lord's Candle

Features: There are many different species of perennial yucca, but the most common in Southern California are Spanish bayonet *(Y. schidigera)*, and Our Lord's candle *(Y. whipplei)*. They both have a large, initial cluster of long narrow yucca leaves with sharp, pointed tips. From the center of this cluster of leaves rises a thick, asparagus-like flower stalk. Spanish bayonet flower stalks grow 3 to 15 feet tall, and those of Our Lord's candle grow 4 to 8 feet tall. The delicate white flowers of our Lord's candle are smaller than the purple-edged, white flowers of Spanish bayonet. Both yuccas have green, capsule-like fruit.

Facts: Yuccas are found in desert areas and piñyon-juniper forests throughout the Southwest and in similar environments worldwide. Their leaves are very fibrous. Native Americans used this fiber to make sandals, twine, nets, burden baskets, etc. Haitians use "sisal" fiber from *Agave sisalana* to make twine. Roots of some of the yuccas contain saponins and can be pounded and soaked in water to make soapsuds. Navajos traditionally use this "soap" as a shampoo for girls at their coming-of-age ceremonies..

Foods:
Raw: Spring flowers from yuccas can be eaten raw, but some taste better than others. Spanish bayonet flowers are some of the tastiest. Be sure to eat only the petals and not the centers of the flowers because the centers are bitter. Some of the fruit can also be eaten raw, but it tastes better cooked.

Cooked: Ripe summer fruit can be peeled and boiled for 10 minutes or baked for 20 minutes at 300°. It tastes good sliced and served with melted butter, or lemon-flavored butter. The flowers, without their centers, can be added to omelets and soups, or boiled

15 to 20 minutes and served with vinegar or butter. Fruits from some varieties of yucca taste better than others. Flavor may vary depending on location, rainfall, soil, and time of year. Flower stalks, picked before the flowers develop, are starchy and can be cooked like potatoes. Native Americans roast the lower 1 to 2 feet of young stalks all day in underground pits. These pits are lined with leaves, filled with hot rocks, and covered with leaves and branches. Yucca stalks are available from spring until summer. The roots are delicious boiled or baked. An average-sized root takes 1 hour to bake, or 45 minutes to boil. Some South Sea islanders like to boil them in coconut milk. The seeds, which contain calcium, can be boiled while they are still white, young, and tender.

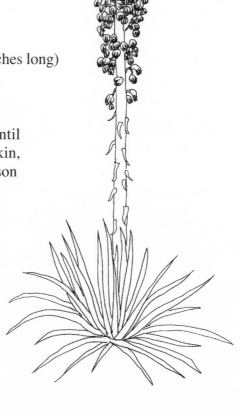

BOILED YUCCA ROOTS
(Serves 4)

> 2 yucca roots (about 8 inches long)
> Butter
> Salt and pepper

Boil roots in a covered pot until tender—about 45 minutes. Skin, slice, and serve with butter. Season with salt and pepper. (If yuccas are endangered where you live, please don't dig them up. You can usually purchase yucca roots at a grocery store).

157

Black Sage
page 12

Blackberry
page 14

Buckwheat
page 16

Bulrush
page 18

Cattail
page 20

White Bark
Ceanothus
page 22

Ceanothus
page 22

Cheeseweed
page 24

Chia
page 26

Chickweed
page 28

Chokecherry
page 30

Chufa
page 32

Cleavers
page 34

Clover
page 36

Sweet Clover
page 36

Cottonwood
page 38

Creosote
page 40

Curly Dock
page 42

Currant
page 44

Dandelion
page 46

Elderberry
page 48

Ephedra
page 50

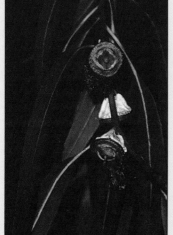

Eucalyptus
page 52

Fiddlehead
page 54

Glasswort
page 56

Goldenrod
page 58

Goldenrod
page 58

Hooker's
Evening Prim-
rose
page 60

Lamb's Quarters
page 62

Lamb's Quarters,
#2
page 64

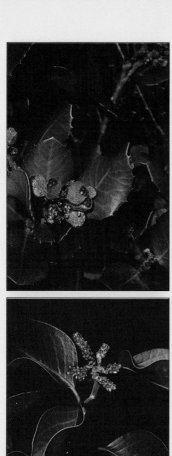

Lemonadeberry
page 66

Squaw Bush
page 66

Sugar Bush
page 66

London Rocket
page 68

Manzanita
page 70

Mesquite
page 72

Milkweed
page 74

Miner's Lettuce
page 76

Mint
page 78

Monkey Flower
page 80

Mullein
page 82

Mustard
page 84

Nasturtium
page 86

Coast Scrub
Oak
page 88

Scrub Oak
page 88

Orach
page 90

Pineapple Weed
page 92

Plantain
page 94

Prickly Lettuce
page 96

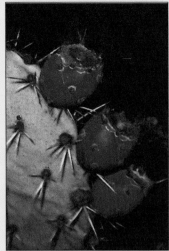

Prickly Pear
page 98

Prickly Sow
Thistle
page 100

Prostrate Pig-
weed
page 102

Purslane
page 104

Serviceberry
page 106

Shepherd's Purse
page 108

Sour Grass
page 110

Sow Thistle
page 112

Stinging Nettle
page 114

Stork's Bill
page 116

Strawberry
page 118

Sweet Fennel
page 120

Thimbleberry
page 122

Thistle
page 124

Toyon
page 126

Tumbleweed
page 128

Veronica
page 130

Watercress
page 132

White Sage
page 134

Wild Celery
page 136

Wild Grape
page 138

Wild Radish
page 140

Wild Rose
page 142

Willow
page 144

Wooly Blue
Curls
page 146

Yarrow
page 148

Yerba Mansa
page 150

Yerba Santa
page 152

Yucca
page 154

California Pepper Tree page 174

Castor Bean page 176 ☠

Cocklebur page 178 ☠

Coyote Melon page 180

False Hellebore page 182 ☠

Jimson Weed page 184 ☠

Lupine
page 186

Mistletoe
page 188

Nightshade
page 190

Poison Oak
page 192

Tree Tobacco
page 194

Turkey Mullein
page 196

PART II

Poisonous Plants

If there is any question about a plant being edible or poisonous, please use extreme caution and do not pick or eat the plant until you know it's safe.

CALIFORNIA PEPPER TREE

Schinus molle

Features: Stately California pepper trees can grow up to 45 feet high. Younger trees are characterized by shaggy, peeling, golden-brown bark laid in overlapping strips. Older bark turns grayish-brown. Numerous pointed, smooth-edged, dull green leaflets grow opposite each other along long, graceful, hanging stems. These are joined by drooping, loose clusters of small yellowish-white flowers which mature into seeds. Beneath their papery, rose-colored husks, the round hard seeds are a dull brown, becoming black as they mature. These seeds are sometimes mistaken for an edible variety of pepper.

Facts: Pepper trees favor slightly moist locations and are often found growing near shallow stream beds. They're common on western ranges from San Diego northward to southern Oregon. They are not native but come from Peru. Legend has it that a grievously ill Spanish sailor was nursed back to health at a California mission. In gratitude, after he returned home, the sailor shipped two pepper trees to the mission for beauty and shade. At first the fathers forgot about the two trees, but eventually they planted them. One of the trees thrived in California's gentle climate. It was very prolific, and most of the pepper trees in California are said to be descended from that very same tree!

WARNING

Although the seeds of this tree resemble peppercorns, they are not edible. Edible peppercorns and ground pepper come from an East Indian pepper vine. Pepper seeds from California pepper trees are considered toxic even though people have been known to consume small amounts of them with no apparent harm.

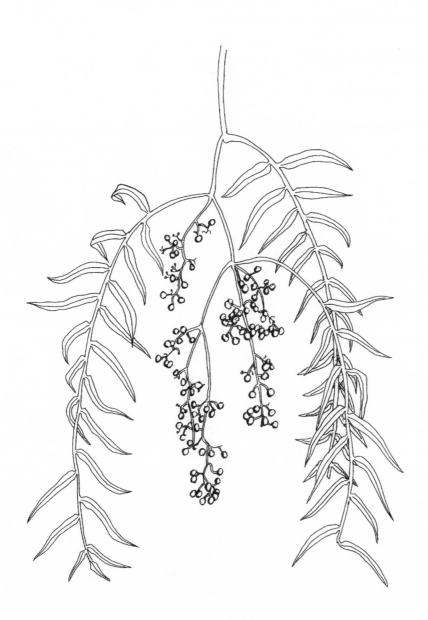

CASTOR BEAN

Ricinus communis

Castor Oil Plant

Features: Castor bean plants, which can be annual or perennial, are large spectacular shrubs or small trees that can grow from 4 to 8 feet tall! They usually have red stems and huge, deeply-lobed, palmate leaves which have 5 to 11 lobes. An unusual feature of castor bean plants is that they have 2 different kinds of flowers growing on the same flower stalks. Small, 3-petaled red flowers grow packed together near the top, and tiny white flowers grow lower down. The fruit of the castor bean is a green, spiny, large gumball-sized capsule which turns brown as it matures. Inside each capsule are 3 bean-sized seeds which resemble small pinto beans in size and shape, but are mottled tan and brown in color.

Facts: Members of this family are common in the tropics. Castor beans grow on disturbed ground or near streambeds in warm regions throughout the world. They contain castor oil which can be used as a laxative after the poison present is neutralized by thorough heating. Because there is a lot of oil in the stalks, they have often been used as torches by such diverse groups as Roman soldiers in Europe and poor people on the island of Brava, one of the Cape Verde islands off the coast of Africa.

WARNING

The inside of castor bean seeds is deadly. Children have been known to die after ingesting as few as 2 or 3. Surprisingly, other people have swallowed these same seeds with impunity, using them as a laxative. This was possible because they swallowed the seeds intact, without breaking the skin. The leaves are also poisonous. Recently, the death of a local horse was attributed to the consumption of castor bean leaves.

<<<177>>>

COCKLEBUR

Xanthium strumarium

Features: Annual cockleburs are sturdy branching plants that grow up to 4 feet high. They are characterized by brown, prickly, velcro-like fruit that attaches itself to anything with which it comes in contact. Stout stems are covered with small hairs and often have purple splotches or lines running along their lengths. Large, abrasive, heart-shaped cocklebur leaves are dark green on top, somewhat lighter beneath, and grow alternately along stems. Cocklebur is often confused with burdock (Arctium minus), which is edible. Both produce burs, but burdock burs are round; whereas cocklebur burs are oval and have 2 small hooks on one end. They also have different flowers. Burdock flowers are purple; cocklebur flowers are greenish-white and smaller.

Facts: Cockleburs grow in dry riverbeds, fields, and waste places throughout the world.

WARNING

Cocklebur plants are poisonous. The young plants and germinating seeds are most dangerous, but the entire plant contains a poisonous chemical called xanthostrumarin, which is lethal when consumed in large quantities.

COYOTE MELON

Cucurbita foetidissima

Buffalo Gourd, Wild Gourd, Calabazilla

Features: Coyote melon plants are prolific perennial vines with stems extending up to 20 feet along the ground, often rooting at the joints. If there are trees or fences in the path of these vines, they will sometimes climb right over them. The large, usually dust-covered green leaves are arrow-shaped, growing up to 20 inches long. These leaves are hairy underneath and have a fetid odor, especially after a good rain. The somewhat fuzzy green gourds have yellow stripes, becoming sand-colored as they age and dry up. They're about the size and shape of slightly flattened oranges. Touching any part of this plant will leave a lingering unpleasant odor on your hand.

Facts: Coyote melons grow in dry gravely places, deserts, and coastal sage scrub from California to Texas. Amazingly, ingenious Native Americans found uses for these gourds, and methods for cooking them. After the "melons" were dried for 2 to 4 months, the seeds were removed and dried. Then the seeds, which contain 25 to 30 percent protein, were fried in oil or ground up and cooked with water to make mush. It is surmised that Pueblo Indians ate the flowers as well as the seeds. They also extracted oil from the roasted seeds which they used for cooking and as a hair conditioner. Coyote melon gourds and leaves are so noxious that they have been used with good results as insect repellents. Because the melons contain saponins, (soap-like compounds), their insides were mashed, boiled, and used to wash clothes.

WARNING

These gourds contain foul-smelling chemicals called cucurbitacins. They are so unfit to eat that people who attempt to eat them without proper preparation; are often nauseous for several hours, experience severe stomach cramps for several days, and suffer diarrhea even longer. Over consumption of coyote melons has proven fatal to sheep and cattle.

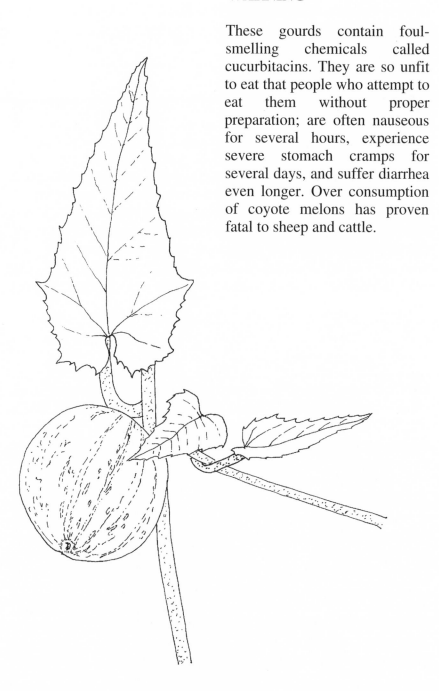

FALSE HELLEBORE

Veratrum californicum

Corn Lily

Features: False hellebore is an erect unbranched perennial that grows 3 to 7 feet high. The mature plant resembles a corn stalk. Large ribbed leaves, 6 to 15 inches long, grow alternately along the stalk. Newer, smaller leaves hug the stalk, but the larger, lower leaves tend to curve away from it. Small, dull, grayish-white flowers grow in long, drooping, terminal clusters at the top of the stalk. As it ages, false hellebore turns golden brown, dries up, and then falls over. Young false hellebore is often mistaken for skunk cabbage, which is edible. Although their leaves resemble each other in size and shape, it is not difficult to distinguish between them. The veins on skunk cabbage leaves branch out from a center spine, but the veins on false hellebore's leaves are vertical— running from top to bottom. Once false hellebore's stalk rises from among its cluster of young leaves, there can no longer be any question as to its identity.

Facts: False hellebore grows in swamps and other moist locations scattered throughout the United States. Surprisingly, some Native Americans have been known to use its roots medicinally. The Shoshones used the raw roots as a snakebite remedy and powdered the dried roots for snuff.

WARNING

All parts of this plant are poisonous. It contains alkaloids which can slow your heart and lower blood pressure. Many years ago, there was a hiker who got lost and hungry near Yosemite. Some false hellebore roots looked pretty good to him, so he took just a few bites. Over the next few days he hallucinated, had blurry vision, vomited, and had diarrhea. By the time he was found he was severely dehydrated! False hellebore does not agree with insects either. Its roots can be powdered and used as an insecticide.

JIMSON WEED

Datura meleloides

Sacred Datura, Toloache

Features: Jimson weed is a common sprawling perennial which grows from 2 to 5 feet tall. Its alternating leaves are a muted dark green and have irregularly toothed margins. The large, lovely, conspicuous white or pale purple trumpet-shaped flowers resemble huge morning glory blooms. These flowers grow singly at the top of short erect flower stems. They open up when it's cool and close during the hottest part of the day. Spiny, green, golf-ball sized jimson weed fruit, which grow along the branches, become brown as they age. Fruit and flowers sometimes appear simultaneously on the plants.

Facts: Sacred datura grows in fields and along roadsides throughout the United States and in similar environments elsewhere. Traditionally, several groups of Native Americans used a tea made from the roots of toloache in the coming-of-age ceremonies for young men. This tea was prepared by medicine men who knew what they were doing. After drinking the tea, the young men would experience a trancelike state for several days, during which time they saw visions. Sometimes people who want to get "high" try to duplicate this tea—often with fatal results.

WARNING

All parts of jimson weed are potentially lethal. Even the fumes from broken plants have been known to make people feel lightheaded.

<<<185>>>

LUPINE

Lupinus longifolius

Bush Lupine, Wolf Pea

Features: There are over 82 different species of lupine in California alone. Some are annual and some are perennial. Although a few are edible if prepared properly, most varieties are poisonous. *Lupinus longifolius* is an upright annual with palmately compound leaves. Most of these leaves grow on individual stems which join with the flower stem at its base, but a few smaller leaves grow along the flower stem, decreasing in size as they approach the flowers. These small, pale, blue-violet flowers resemble pea flowers and form whorls along the ends of the flower stalks. Other varieties of lupine have flowers which are yellow, blue, purple, red or white. Lupine seeds grow in stiff pods which look like small, slightly hairy, pea pods. The leaves are also hairy with soft silky hairs beneath. Some varieties of lupine appear dull green in color, punctuated by their lovely blossoms.

Facts: Lupines grow on hillsides, in pastures, open spaces, and coastal sage and scrub chaparral habitats from the Arctic to California, and in other countries as well. They're useful plants to have around. Not only are lupines attractive without requiring much water or maintenance, but they enrich the soil with nitrogen.

WARNING

Many species of lupine contain alkaloid poisons. These poisons are most concentrated in the seedpods. Alkaloids can severely inflame stomachs and intestines. Although some lupines have been eaten safely, others are known to have poisoned cattle and sheep. Because lupines hybridize freely, it is often difficult to distinguish between edible and non-edible varieties.

<<<187>>>

MISTLETOE

Phoradendron villosum

Features: Mistletoe is a green parasitic plant which hangs in large clusters of drooping branches from its host trees, usually oak or sycamore. One variety of mistletoe, called "juniper mistletoe," grows on juniper trees. Mistletoe leaves are thick, smooth-edged, and somewhat ovate or spoon-shaped. They grow opposite each other along short branches on small individual stems and form clusters at their tips. Mistletoe produces tiny white berries which are eaten by birds.

Facts: *Phoradendron villosum* grows in California, Mexico, Oregon, and Texas. Some Navajos in Utah used to eat juniper mistletoe. They steamed the entire plant, berries and all. Although most Native Americans did not attempt to consume any variety of mistletoe, some cooked the entire plant to make a treatment for lice and dandruff. Most people only recognize mistletoe at Christmas time when it is traditionally hung over doorways so that young men have an excuse to kiss young ladies who "accidentally" stand under it. Birds inadvertently help propagate mistletoe by eating the berries and then recycling the seeds at their next perch. They also transport the sticky berries which cling to their legs.

WARNING

All parts of mistletoe are poisonous. It contains chemicals which cause veins to constrict and increase blood pressure.

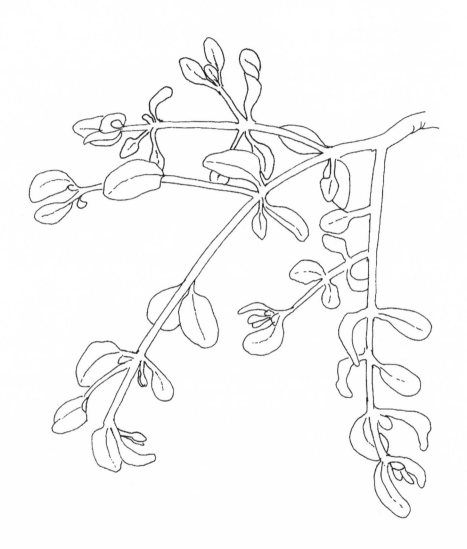

NIGHTSHADE

Solanum xantii

Purple Nightshade

Solanum douglasii

Features: There are over 100 different species of nightshade, many of which are poisonous. Pictured on the left *is Solanum xantii,* which is easily recognized by its disc-like, 5-lobed, purple flowers that appear as if the 5 petals are joined together. In the center of these flowers are dark green spots and a beak-like cone of yellow anthers. *S. douglasii,* (pictured on the right), whose berries can be eaten if prepared properly, has small, white, 5-petaled flowers. Prolific purple nightshade is a graceful, branched perennial which adorns shady chaparral locations with its colorful flowers. Growing up to several feet high, it sometimes supports itself, vine-like, on other plants or trees. Oval leaves, each on a separate stem, grow alternately along the stalk. Purple flowers form small clusters near the tips of the branches and are followed by small green berries which turn dark purple as they ripen.

Facts: Nightshade plants can be found in dry or moist open woods and waste areas throughout the United States. Solanum is a large plant family which includes a surprising number of plants we commonly eat, such as; tomatoes, potatoes, peppers, and eggplant. Their leaves and potato vines are all poisonous. Tomatoes used to be called "Devil's apples." Thomas Jefferson was the first colonist to promote them as food. Cooking neutralizes some of the poisons. Both settlers and Native Americans ate the fully ripe berries of *S. douglasii* after cooking them but did not attempt to eat berries from other species. Native Americans used juice from nightshade berries to make a dye and to cure inflamed eyes. Tobacco is another member of the solanum family.

WARNING

Many of these species contain dangerous alkaloids. Nicotine and atropine are two of them. These alkaloids have a quieting effect on the respiratory system and can be toxic if taken in excess.

Solanum xantii

Solanum douglasii

POISON OAK

Toxicodendron diversilobum

Features: Pernicious poison oak can be a small deciduous plant, a shrub, or a climbing vine. It's recognized by its sets of 3 leaflets with the 2 side leaflets touching near their bases and a central leaflet on a slightly extended stem. These leaves, which grow 1 1/2 to 8 inches long, are usually green with a shiny coating of an oil irritant. In autumn, they often turn a lovely shade of red, tempting unwary admirers to pick them. Drooping clusters of tiny, inconspicuous, greenish-white flowers are followed by round white berries. People have been known to confuse blackberry plants with poison oak because of their similar leaves. The most obvious differences are the presence of thorns on blackberry bushes, and the extended central leaflet of poison oak.

Facts: Poison oak grows in moist shady locations throughout the West. Native Americans are often said to be immune to poison oak, yet they have numerous cures for it. One of their best-known cures was to eat a few of the young leaves at the beginning of poison oak season. There are mixed reports on the effectiveness of this cure. Some people claim that it works; whereas others say that it has caused painful outbreaks of poison oak blisters in and around their mouths! Prevention is the best cure. Stay away from poison oak!

WARNING

Poison oak leaves are coated with a nonvolatile oil called urushiol. Many people are allergic to this oil. Within 24 hours of coming into contact with it they break out in itchy, watery blisters and rashes which are sometimes painful. These symptoms can last anywhere from a few days to several months. Even the fumes from burning poison oak are toxic and present a real health hazard to firefighters. Poison oak oil retains its potency for extensive periods of time. I personally contracted a severe case of poison oak after borrowing a friend's sleeping bag which had been in contact with poison oak over a month previously. There is a "suburban legend" about a family who gathered lovely red poison oak vines and filled their car with them. The whole family caught poison oak. They treated their problem, but forgot to clean the car. The next time they rode in it they caught poison oak all over again!

TREE TOBACCO

Nicotiana glauca

Features: Tree tobacco is a small, fast-growing tree which reaches heights of 6 to 20 feet. The large, muted blue-green leaves are soft in texture and oval in shape. Long, tubular, greenish-yellow flowers grow in drooping clusters at the end of the branches. Tree tobacco does not require a lot of water and thrives in waste places.

Facts: Tree tobacco is common throughout the Southwest, especially along washes and in waste places below 3,000 feet. Both Native Americans and settlers used the leaves for smoking. Native Americans also used this tree medicinally, steaming the leaves for a poultice or placing them fresh inside a moccasin to relieve tired feet. Their children knew how to suck on the base of the flowers to enjoy their sweetness without ingesting any poison. Sometimes people mistakenly call tree tobacco "Indian Tobacco," but this name is traditionally applied to several smaller members of the nicotiana family. Therefore, it's best not to refer to tree tobacco by this name.

WARNING

Tree tobacco is poisonous raw or cooked because it has a high nicotine content, especially the leaves. People have been known to die after eating tree tobacco leaves.

TURKEY MULLEIN

Eremocarpus setigerus

Features: Turkey mullein is a low-growing, prostrate, spreading annual. It grows only 5 to 8 inches high and often forms mats. The entire plant is pale gray-green and fuzzy. The leaves are ovate with pointed tips, growing in stiff clusters consisting of several leaves of various sizes. Inconspicuous bunches of tiny yellow flowers grow in the center of the leaf clusters.

Facts: Turkey mullein grows inland from the coast in dry waste places, along roadsides, in grasslands, oak woods, coastal sage and scrub, on mountains west of the Sierras, and near deserts from southern California north to Washington. It is called turkey mullein and dove weed because turkeys and doves are both very fond of the seeds. This can be misleading because another plant, *Croton texensis,* is also known as dove weed. Turkey mullein contains a narcotic poison that was used by Native Americans to catch fish. After crushing the plant they threw it into shallow streams or ponds. Stunned fish rose to the surface where they were easily gathered. Native Americans also used turkey mullein to poison their arrow tips.

WARNING

As a member of the euphorbias, turkey mullein is related to other potentially poisonous plants. Some harmful chemicals it contains are: eremone, b-pinene, myrcene, and trans-ethyl-cinnamate. Even though turkey mullein can't be used for food, it can still be used medicinally. A poultice made from the leaves is reputed to relieve internal chest pains and a decoction of the leaves in warm water was sometimes used to help with asthma and fevers.

PLANT SUBSTITUTION APPENDIX

Interchangeable Mild-flavored Plants

Wild	Domestic
Amaranth	Spinach
Amaranth, #2	Swiss chard
Lamb's quarters	Beet greens
Lamb's quarters, #2	
Miner's lettuce	
Orach (use less salt)	
Prostrate pigweed	
Sow thistle	
Stinging nettle	

Interchangeable Bitter or Strong-flavored Plants

Wild	Domestic
Dandelion	Mustard greens
London rocket	Turnip greens
Mustard	Collard greens
Nasturtium (use less)	
Watercress	

BIBLIOGRAPHY

Arvigo, Rosita, Balick, Michael. Rainforest Remedies, Lotus Press, Twin Lakes, Wisconsin, 1993.

Balls, Edward K. Early Uses of California Plants, University of California Press, Berkeley and Los Angeles, 1962.

Bean, Lowell John, Saubel, Katherine Siva. Temalpakh, Malki Museum Press, Banning, California, 1972, 1979, 1982, 1987.

Boxer, Arabella, and Back, Philippa. The Herb Book, Peerage Books, London, 1987, 1988.

Brackett, Babette, and Lash, Maryanne. The Wild Gourmet, David R. Bodine, Publisher, Boston, 1975.

Bremness, Lesley. R D Home Handbooks/Herbs, The Reader's Digest Association, Inc., New York, 1990.

Clarke, Charlotte Bringle. Edible and Useful Plants of California, The University of California Press, Berkeley and Los Angeles, 1977.

Dale, Nancy. Flowering Plants, The Santa Monica Mountains, Coastal and Chaparral Regions of Southern California, Capra Press, Santa Barbara, 1985.

Dunmire, William W., Tierney, Gail D., Wild Plants of the Pueblo Province, Museum of New Mexico Press, Santa Fe, New Mexico, 1995.

Editors of Alaska Magazine. Alaska Wild Berry Guide and Cookbook, Alaska Northwest Publishing Co., Anchorage, Alaska, 1982.

Genders, Roy. Edible Wild Plants, A Guide to Natural Foods, Van Der Marck Editions, New York, 1988.

Graham, Frances Kelso. Plant Lore of an Alaskan Island, Alaskan Northwest Publishing Company, Anchorage, 1985.

Hall, Alan. The Wild Food Trail Guide, Holt, Rinehart, and Winston, New York, 1973, 1976.

Harrington, H. D. Western Edible Plants, The University of New Mexico Press, Albuquerque, 1967, 1984.

Hedges, Ken. Santa Ysabel Ethnobotany, San Diego Museum of Man, San Diego, 1986.

Kirk, Donald R. Wild Edible Plants of Western North America, Naturegraph Publishers, Inc., Happy Camp, California, 1970, 1975.

Kotzen, Alice. Malki Museum's Native Food Testing Experience, Malki Museum, Banning, California, 1994.

Larkcom, Joy. The Salad Garden, The Viking Press, New York, 1984.

Munz, Philip A. A Flora of Southern California, University of California Press, Berkeley and Los Angeles, 1974.

Niethammer, Carolyn. American Indian Food and Lore, Macmillan Publishing Company, New York, 1974.

Niethammer, Carolyn. The Tumbleweed Gourmet. Tucson: University of Arizona Press, 1987.

Schofield, Janice J. Discovering Wild Plants, Alaska Northwest Books, Anchorage, 1989.

Stewart, Jon Mark. Colorado Desert Wildflowers, Self-published, Singapore, 1993.

Sweet, Muriel. Common Edible and Useful Plants of the West, Naturegraph Publishers, Inc., Happy Camp, California, 1976.

Wiltens, James. Plants Your Mother Never Told You About, Deer Crossing Camp Press, Cupertino, California, 1986.

INDEX

Kahanah Farnsworth is a credentialed teacher and outdoor educator who lives in Southern California. In this book she has combined her love of the outdoors, interest in ethnobotany, skill in cooking, and pleasure in writing and drawing. We hope that you will enjoy reading and using *A Taste of Nature* as much as she has enjoyed writing it.